I can give you anything but love

I CAN GIVE YOU ANYTHING BUT LOVE

G★A★R★Y
INDIANA

SEVEN STORIES PRESS
NEW YORK • OAKLAND • LONDON

For Jerry Gorovoy and Tracey Emin

Naturally, at first it would only be a troublesome, tiring work, it wouldn't stop me from existing or feeling that I exist. But a time would come when the book would be written, when it would be behind me, and I think that a little of its clarity might fall over my past. Then, perhaps, because of it, I could remember my life without repugnance. Perhaps one day, thinking precisely of this hour, of this gloomy hour in which I wait, stooping, for it to be time to get on the train, perhaps I shall feel my heart beat faster and say to myself: "That was the day, that was the hour, when it all started." And I might succeed—in the past, nothing but the past—in accepting myself.

Jean-Paul Sartre, *Nausea*

In the Philippines, almost every week, someone is killed in a karaoke bar for singing "My Way," by someone else who doesn't like his singing. "My Way" is, of course, a hubristic and self-congratulating song, as many Frank Sinatra standards are. But "My Way" is a particularly abrasive song for people who have to listen to someone else singing it. A person who thinks he did it his way is often mistaken, but even if he really did, it's sometimes prudent not to sing about it.

one

This afternoon Abdul showed up at my apartment on Calle 21 y G. In the door's judas eye I made out a sweat-beaded face from an old photo, scarily close and unexpected, like a sea monster humping a periscope. At first I couldn't tell if he was Abdul or another mulatto who boned me a few times a thousand years ago, when the skin market assembled at night by the Fiat garage on the Malecón. The other guy went *loco* the summer a drug shipment slipped past the coast guard and flooded Havana with cocaine. Before that, even a little weed was a shrieking rarity. By September, *jineteros* were burgling houses for coke money and banging clients in apartment-house doorways.

After an inevitable crackdown, gay rights groups in El Norte denounced the Castro regime's repressive measures. The Castro regime can piss up a rope, but some repressive measures are understandable. Nightlife shifted up La Rampa and the hustlers took over the cafetería at 23 y G, a block from where I am now. Then when I was away for seven years the scene trickled back to the Malecón. The Bim Bom cafetería at La Rampa and Infante is homo central these days. The old Fiat dealership has become a spruced-up café serving breakfast at sidewalk tables.

I wouldn't want to see the cokehead again. I didn't feature seeing Abdul much, either. I don't like people showing up here uninvited. It's important to maintain boundaries. Besides that, Abdul is a pig. A harmless pig, but a pig all the same. I thought to keep the barred security door between us, then realized it wasn't locked.

"I saw you last night at Bim Bom," he said, flicking the door latch and slipping into the salon. He attempted a hug. I slid out of reach and steered him out to the terrace.

"I followed you up here," he proudly revealed, "but it was dark."

I wasn't sure what he meant by that, exactly. People like Abdul have eyes that see in the dark with the accuracy of night-vision goggles. For that matter, they could pick up your location anywhere in Havana as if your wallet was sending a GPS signal. Some would mistake this for tropical exuberance run awry. Worse, people like Abdul expect congratulations for raping your privacy.

Abdul is an attractive man, now in his thirties. In the US or Europe, he could model underpants for Calvin Klein. There is nothing overtly crass or desperate about him. Still, in days of old, he was full of crude calculation, an annoying self-assurance that emanated from his prick. That hadn't changed, either.

"Why not say something instead of following me?"

He strode to the edge of the terrace and pointed to the Parque Victor Hugo across from the Romanian embassy.

"I would have! A police stopped me, over there."

Like all Havanans, Abdul refers to law enforcement officers using the indefinite article, as one speaks of an invasive plant species.

"Oh. In other words, you followed me for fifteen blocks in the dark."

He pretended not to hear, tapping spatulate fingers on the glass table. He glanced at my notebooks and pencils, then pulled out a metal chair from the table. It screeched horribly against the floor tiles. Seated, he suddenly looked compressed and expectant, somebody waiting for a bus, or a doctor.

"Why you didn't come all these years?"

"*Porque . . . porque yo estaba tan feliz aqui la ultima vez.*" It's hard to sell sarcasm in a second language. I didn't succeed, or else he wasn't having any. I was happy here when he last saw me, actually. At times.

"*¿Que?*"

"*Porque despues de Nine Eleven, el gobierno de los Estados Unidos lo hizo impossible.*"

"*Si, claramente, entiendo.*"

Do Cubans call "9/11" *Nueve Once*? Or something else? What Americans call the Bay of Pigs, Cubans call the Victory of Giron. Maybe they have less apocalyptically compressed terms for disasters befalling El Norte, which Americans consider infinitely worse than anybody else's. It was a pivotal event in the modern world, obviously. But Cuba hasn't been part of the modern world in a long time, marooned in a Marxist-Leninist time warp of sluggish totalitarianism.

I poured Havana Club and cola into a pitcher while citing punitive measures the US can take against unlicensed travelers if it wishes, notably a twenty-five-thousand dollar fine. Not worth talking about, but I was never in the habit of conversation with Abdul. When I knew him before, I spoke about ten words of Spanish. Being fluent now didn't change things. Flutters of comprehension involving his chin and fingers as he drained his glass didn't convince me he had any idea what I was talking about. In Abdul's particular milieu, it's never clear if people even try to follow what you're saying, or listen for key words while waiting to bring money into the conversation.

It felt confusing to see him. A little sad. The connection was never important enough to joyfully recall it a decade later. I didn't suppose he was in throes of fond remembrance, either. Yet we acted like old friends who had liked each other a great deal more than we actually had. Abdul isn't old enough to find the continued existence of another person uncanny, I thought. One has to lose quite a few people before that happens. Maybe he senses something encouraging in the fact that I'm not dead by now, but he isn't surprised. It surprises me, but that's a whole other story.

There was nothing to do but show him the kitchen, the back terrace looking down Calle G, where it stretches to the Caribbean, passing the Hotel Presidente and the tall buildings on the Malecón. The smaller bathroom. The middle bedroom. The long blue-tiled bathroom between the bedrooms. The front bedroom with shuttered French windows that open on the narrow part of the front terrace. I keep valuables in the spare bedroom closet and dresser drawers. I learned the folly of renting a flat without a locked safe room a long time ago. Abdul doesn't steal, I recalled. Out of habit, though, and in case, I told him it was a storage room, that the owner in Bogotá has the key.

He ogled the flat with blatant territorial lust. Everything visibly scrubbed, swept, mopped, dusted, washed, folded, and tucked into place, daily. Palatial rooms, bare looking despite many paintings and lots of heavy mahogany furniture. An enviable residence by Havana standards, though many grander ones exist, not only in Vedado and west of here in Miramar, but even in Casablanca, across the port tunnel, or the slummy outlying districts east of Habana Vieja like Regla and Cerro. In every quarter, houses

built for the rich who fled half a century ago were
redistributed after the Revolution, parceled into *ciudadela*
or left intact for single families. You'd have to be a
determined swine not to see something wonderful about
this, considering who owned these houses under Batista.
"There was a man who loved islands," the D. H.
Lawrence story begins. "He was born on one, but it didn't
suit him, as there were too many other people on it, besides
himself." It was said of D. H. Lawrence that he never
believed in the existence of other people, and when he was
forced to, he hated them. Well. There is, aside from that,
this thing about islands: unlike the whole world, an island
is a place a solitary person can attempt to understand.

This city was built for giant people with histrionic lives,
the bygone lives portrayed in the Brazilian *telenovelas*
everybody watches here; lives magnified by vertiginous
ceilings and endless marble-floored rooms. Many not-well-
off Cubans with lives of lesser grandeur inhabit the weather-
beaten villas of vanished gangsters and deposed politicians
with a casual dignity that isn't entirely borrowed from a
different time and a higher class. They have as much
ancestral memorabilia as their former overlords, and often
more impressive family histories, educational credentials,
and professional attainments. That's how it is.

The flats in this building, and the identical house beside
it on Calle 21, are occupied—or unoccupied—by professionals
who leave the island whenever they please. It's not merely
the flat that's enviable, though it's nicer than where many
of my friends live, but also the privilege implied by the
owner's perennial absence, the working elevator, the copious
unused space. At least two flats in this house have been
empty as long as I can remember, their owners working
abroad and unlikely ever to live here again.

The apartment is riddled with mirrors. An absurdly huge one framed in polished mahogany in the front bedroom, smaller ones in the bathrooms, mirrored insets in cabinets, mirrors placed strategically over bureaus and dressers to primp and knot ties in, or reflect a much-enacted primal scene. Alberto, who owns this flat and its twin in the adjacent building wing, and another on the top floor, is a famous Cuban actor currently working in soaps shot in Colombia: *A Corazón Abierto, La Quiero a Morir, Milagros de Amor.* His old Communist father occupies the flat directly overhead, under the roof. He's senile. Each summer, Alberto leases the next-door place to an aunt who lives in Madrid. Alberto painted the pictures on the walls. He is highly esteemed as a painter in Cuba, besides being a famous actor. I don't know what to say about these paintings, except that they look very Cuban.

Because Alberto and his family enjoy gazing at themselves (their names are carved in the fieldstone half-wall of the front terrace; I picture them grouped inside the largest mirror, arrayed in lace mantillas and brocade morning coats from another century, or from an episode of *Milagros de Amor*, figures in a Sargent painting), the deflating evidence of passing time snags my attention when I pass through the rooms. Time is glacially slow in this country, but my face races on, across all the mirrors, en route to the eternity of nothingness behind the finish line.

More or less by chance, I've ascended a few rungs of the local social ladder since my long-ago rental on Principe Street, where Ricardo and Barbara Marcet live. Which is where I had the long-ago affair with Abdul, among others. I've lived in this new place, sporadically, for two years. Abdul is the only person from that earlier time I've encountered. One day I will visit Ricardo and Barbara. I

know I've avoided them because Principe Street will be
another mirror reminding me how days become months
and months become years. I didn't know what to tell Abdul
about all the time gone missing, about the money I once
had evaporating like steam, or the terrifying movements
of clocks when you start to be old.

Nueve Once had nothing to do with it, really. The
American travel ban was ramped up, or so I was told, and
the hysteria of those months and years probably deflected
me from the effort coming back here would have required,
in my suddenly reduced circumstances. A more pedestrian
reason was a publishing lunch in 2002, where I was about
to hand across the table a proposal for a book about the
island—one that my editor had informally commissioned,
and dangled a half-million-dollar advance for—when said
editor announced she was leaving the company.

It was a decision obviously reached rather previously.
("Jumped or was pushed," my agent japed that afternoon,
"we'll never know which, either.") It took fantastic effrontery
for her to pretend otherwise, but the betrayal itself was
nothing unusual in the publishing business. After pulling
the plug on my income for what turned out to be a biblical
span, she dragged me to Bergdorf Goodman, where she
laid out two thousand dollars for a handbag.

This came to mind this afternoon because that luncheon,
more than anything else, probably accounts for the great
gap in continuity, almost a geological fissure. Seven or
eight years of spiritual grisaille commenced between the
dessert flan and the custom handbag counter at Bergdorf's.
After those flattening years, Havana no longer seemed the
place to be. But it is. It always has been. This city is my
heart. I will never fully understand why I ever let it go. I
would have been lost trying to squeeze the missing time

through the mangle of my own language, much less explain it in defective Spanish. Abdul wasn't really curious about it, anyway.

I came here with Ferd Eggan in May 2001. That would have been the last time until this afternoon that I saw Abdul, his perfect muscle tone glistening with coconut oil. Naked except for a leather jock strap and cowboy boots, riding a horse behind the dunes at Playa Mi Cayito.

Ferd and I had rented separate cabins at the campgrounds. He had brought along his *jinetero*, who was busy stuffing his face at a kiosk selling food-like substances out on the highway. Stumbling across the grounds on a foot path of dessicated mud that turned into fiery sand and prickling dune grass, we debated driving the next morning along the northern route to Santiago de Cuba, or taking roads that run through Cienfuegos, Trinidad de Cuba, and Camagüey. The customary beauty pageant swarmed over undulating humps of sand: nearly naked young men with perfect bodies catwalking to a parking lot refreshment stand, or back to rented beach umbrellas and plastic chaise lounges spread along the shore.

My nickname for Playa Mi Cayito is Porno Beach. Rent boys who hang around the Malecón at night spend their days there, promoting fantastic endowments against a majestic backdrop of foaming surf and azure skies, wearing the least possible excuses for bathing suits, often improvised from see-through materials. Beachwear magnifies their genitals to Godzilla scale, evoking commedia dell'arte phalluses.

Pingueros I recognize from the city prowl the shore in a state of elephantine tumescence, waggling their groins at likely clients sprawled on chaises and blankets. Most johns are roughly the age of a *pinguero*'s grandfather. In the harsh UV broiler of daylight, the effect of their tribal-looking sunscreen is that of the cold cream with which ancient goddesses of the stage wipe off their makeup after a matinee. Older men at Playa Mi Cayito are obese, emaciated, wasted from chemo, bald, decrepit, ugly, flamboyantly queeny, or several of these things at the same time.

There are some attractive older parties on the beach who arrive there preattached to comely young consorts. If they are well-off and foreign, they're the guys all *pingueros* want to hook up with (though a *pinguero* will settle for just well-off, if need be), hoping for a ticket off the island, some capital to start a business, or a house they will own instead of having to live with their parents.

The faintest sign delivers the desired merchandise to any parasol or blanket. It's simple to make a date. Some *pingueros* will perform anything short of full penetration on the spot. Some will fuck right there in the water.

I'm not wild about Playa Mi Cayito. There are two gray-uniformed cops forever glowering from under a beach umbrella, and they're bad news. They're planted like shrubs for a cop's-eye panorama of the whole beach, easily spotting their victims. Bored and malevolent, they seize selected youths and drag them off to a holding tank a couple miles up the highway. The more aggressive exhibitionists and public sodomites pay them off, the price of a beach cop being two dollars or a beer and a sandwich. Instead, they pick out young guys who aren't soliciting, who came with a "tourist" friend. The police consider any non-Cuban a tourist. There's no law against Cubans fraternizing with tourists, but cops make their own laws everywhere, and here you need to bribe them to leave you alone.

"You feel okay?" Ferd asked.

We had stopped on the way for chicken kebabs and

beers at a roadside stand. Minutes after driving away we had to pull over. I felt my guts trying to spray through my nose. I scrambled out in time to redecorate the road instead of the Lexus upholstery. Now I felt the beach path spinning slightly.

"I'm fine, I think so. It feels like it all came up."

A horse's muzzle snorted beside my head.

Abdul was peering down from the saddle of a pure white quarterhorse gelding. When it registered that it was Abdul, and that the expensively-bred animal he was on was rented to anybody at the beach, twinges of nausea pinched my stomach. I felt sorry for the gelding. Abdul didn't belong on him. Abdul in a jockstrap riding a white horse was a pretty astounding visual, though. He looked like Mellors in a *telenovela* adaptation of Lady Chatterley.

Would I care to meet his mother, he wanted to know. I envisioned a crumbly old slut striking Hollywood poses on a moth-eaten blanket, slathering wrinkled bosoms with tanning oil. I was finished with Abdul. A flicker of curiosity ran through me, but I fought it. I said I'd prefer not.

Six months earlier, I had brought him two pairs of ridiculously pricey Barker Black shoes from the Melrose Avenue Fred Segal's in West Hollywood. One pair pinched his toes when he tried them on. His instant petulance was too brutal a reminder of the cold equation underlying our supposed romance. I only travel with one suitcase and a shoulder bag, ever. Even if I'm going to be gone for months. In most cities of the world, if you need socks or a burner phone you can buy them anywhere. Cuba isn't a consumer society, though, and even in Havana there are shortages of what little there is: you bring what you'll need with you, right down to disposable razors and pencils. Half my luggage consists of things my friends want: sunglasses, shirts, computer batteries, all kinds of provender that's insanely expensive or else nonexistent on the island. Abdul's shoes had taken up a lot of premium space in the suitcase. As I saw it, he should have been pleased to get one set of elegant footwear, and I'd given him two. He could sell them if they didn't fit, for more than he made peddling his *pinga* in a month. I saw that this icy, churlish indignation over the normal tightness of new shoes was going to be his stock reaction to any expensive gift, as if he were some sought-after courtesan from a Balzac novel.

I avoided him after that. When he showed up at Principe Street I didn't let him in. Abdul has his pride. He went away, and stayed away. At Playa Mi Cayito, he stared at me for an uncomfortable minute, then tapped his stirrups on the horse's ribs and cantered off.

I collapsed as Ferd and I strolled back to the cabins hours later. The doctor on call at the park infirmary described it as the worst case of dysentery he'd seen in twenty years. He quickly injected me with three different antibiotics followed by a stiff dose of morphine. A blanket of gelatin sucked me into squishy oblivion until the next day.

This afternoon, Abdul said he opened a *paladar* with his brother in 2008, in Barrio Chino. He lives over the dining room in a flat. It's somewhere on Dragones Street behind the Capitolio. Hard work doesn't get you anywhere in Cuba, but in his case it apparently has.

But not far enough, evidently, since he expected cash after we finished the rum and briefly squirmed through a strictly aerobic fuck—a segue I stupidly didn't see coming and basically resented. Abdul is indifferent to other people's moods and feelings. I thought of the ill-fitting shoes while he pounded away.

"It's a lot more expensive now for me to come here,

you know, with the CUC," I told him, washing his sperm off my face as he lathered his balls in the shower.

The CUC, a convertible peso, is a recent tweak of the island's sad fortunes. Based on nothing but wishes, it's worthless anywhere besides here. When I left in 2001, the standard currency was the US dollar, the sugar economy having collapsed along with the Soviet Union. That was what's called the Special Period, which everyone remembers as utterly, horribly special. There has always been the national peso as well as real money—currently twenty-four Cuban pesos to one CUC, I think—which Cubans freely accept from Cubans but rarely from outsiders. The national peso has magically ample buying power for things like vegetables, chicken, Santeria spells, and Cuban taxis (as opposed to licensed ones). It's useless for buying luxury goods, hotel rooms, anything imported. I'm sure you could counterfeit it with a color Xerox.

"Yes, too bad for you," Abdul said, swiping his still-godlike, visibly older form with a green towel.

"Too bad for you too," I said. "At least if you had any real money, you could leave the country."

A cruel remark, but it flew past him. I resented in advance the time I'd now have to waste deflecting his attentions whenever we ran into each other on the Malecón.

"Those kids at Bim Bom," I said. "It's not like years ago, they're all . . ."

I couldn't think of a Spanish word for *méchant*. Abdul knew what I meant anyway. He isn't stupid.

"There is no other place," he said, "so all kinds go to Bim Bom—*viciosos, mala hierba*, good ones, *criminales*. The boys you like cannot pay to go into Las Vegas Club."

Las Vegas Club is a tiny disco on Infante that features antediluvian drag acts and thirty-year-old music videos, dreary, mirror-ball lighting effects, and an A/C that turns it all into the Patagonian Ice Sheet.

"I didn't come here for that," I said. "I'm old, Abdul. An old man with a boy who is twenty, that is disgusting."

I was lying, but it sounded all right.

Abdul shrugged: whatever.

★

Cesare Pavese: "The only reason why we are always thinking of our own ego is that we have to live with it more continuously than with anyone else's." At some bend in the river, you suddenly realize that questions that have pressed against your skull since the age of reason don't have any answers. None you're ever going to know, anyway. My mother told me more than once that after the incident at the lake I was never the same person as before, but when she said things in the ponderously grave voice she assumed, in very unusual situations, to "really talk" about something, I recognized, in an apathetic way, the family habit of blaming our emotional traumas and deep disappointments on external forces and people we weren't related to.

Our private psychological mess (incessantly churned up not only by my parents, my brother Kev, and me, but also by my mother's numerous siblings, my father's parents, and surprise guest appearances by relatives residing elsewhere) was never acknowledged for what it was: a swamp of human wreckage heavily tainted by alcohol. Reality was never discussed in the open, but brooded over endlessly in our separate mental jail cells. It was an unwritten law that any ugly circumstance was other people's fault; we weren't perfect, and didn't claim to be, but we were a hell of a lot better than other people. Absolutely nothing supported this delusion, aside from a strict observance of three or four of the Ten Commandments that happened to coincide with felony statutes. But there it was.

The incident at the lake happened like this: An instructor at the Derry Park and Recreation Area, Shirley Casey, gave me daily swimming lessons for a few months. She took a keen interest in my progress, held me afloat with maternal firmness in the lake as I learned the various strokes, and treated me for weeks as her special friend out of the twelve or thirteen kids taking lessons from her.

One day, out of the blue, Shirley had the bright idea to attack me, with the help of Bruce Anteyer, the other swimming teacher, a six-foot dude with no personality and a whiffle haircut who strutted up and down the beach with the vigilant expression of Sheriff Matt Dillon on *Gunsmoke*, his turquoise nylon trunks sporting a perpetual boner Shirley had been sucking off all summer behind the arts-and-crafts cottage.

The teen aqua instructors grabbed me from behind while I was watching Kev knock balls around on the badminton court. They dragged me to the lake. Shirley jammed a towel in my mouth while Bruce fastened a blindfold over my eyes, then they helped each other hogtie me with some clothesline.

Next, they carried me to the parks and recreation department's aluminum skiff, dumped me in, rowed to the middle of the lake, and hoisted me onto a raft, where they left me trussed up for several hours. I heard the sporadic creaking of oarlocks, faint splashes of paddles shirring water, as if they were circling the raft at an alarming distance, keeping an eye on my reactions. I also heard unintelligible murmuring, possibly Bruce and Shirley debating what story to tell if I rolled into the water and drowned.

I was eight or nine. Eventually they came back and got me, rowed to the beach, untied me, and removed the gag and blindfold. I ran home in a panic, as if running for the bomb shelter my father kept refusing to build in our basement. My parents were at work. I shook for hours, curled up in a fetal clump under my bed. By the time P and M got home I'd managed to stop shaking and was breathing normally. I didn't say a word. It was too insane to talk about. My brother spilled it when he showed up, in his account pretending he'd gone into town before it started and only got back to the lake after they let me go. He knew he'd be sorry if he didn't tell before they heard about it some other way.

Maybe that flipped me over to the dark side, as per Mumma's preferred narrative. I tend to think I was pushed in that direction by things a lot closer to home.

Plenty of kids witnessed the whole episode, including Kev, of course, who didn't lift a finger to rescue me. The whole town knew about it before Walter Cronkite and the news hour came on. Mumma knew who to call and what to tell them. Bruce and Shirley found themselves instantly unemployed, banned forever from the recreation area.

If it had been the custom, my mother would have pressed charges, and sued the town for a million dollars. She was fiercely protective. What Bruce and Shirley had done was so creepy that even people who couldn't stand my family called to say how sympathetic and upset they were. In the 1950s, though, where I came from, if something awful happened to you, you sucked it up, regardless of what "it" was. Gross medical malpractice, head-on highway collision, termination of employment without cause.

Violent bullying was an ordinary feature of school. I was what bigger kids called a shrimp, threateningly brainy, and a bit of a sissy too, so I came in for a lot. This assault was only a topic because nobody could figure out why it happened. Shirley Casey's sister married Mumma's cousin Billy Peyton years later. She said their family never got to the bottom of it either. Apparently Shirley herself couldn't come up with any reason. It had just sort of happened.

I have no idea how Shirley Casey's life turned out. As far as the place where I grew up is concerned, Janis Joplin said it as well as I could, when somebody asked her about being laughed out of Port Arthur, Texas: "They're all back there, plumbers just like they were." Except by now, I suppose, most of them are dead.

I can't recall that faraway period in any fine detail, much less what I thought about what happened to me. When people refer to "the benefit of hindsight" they forget that hindsight is the back end of a firearm, not some elevated wisdom they've acquired from their childhood nightmares.

I've never felt like writing about childhood. Memoirs invariably open in some bygone era. I'm old enough to justify writing about my history, but too old to remember much of it. It's one thing to make things up, but painting specifics that are only guesses feels like fraud. My memory is a viscid, opaque continuum of fragments: horses, adventures on my bicycle, bloody scrapes from skating mishaps, skiing into a tree under the lift at Mount Sunapee, digging clams at Orchard Beach. There isn't a hope of answering any questions I have about anything. The few survivors from that place and period don't remember the same things I do, or remember them all differently.

What else was happening in the frame while Robert, my cousin-godmother Ellen's brother, taught me to play chess in their mother's living room in Augusta, Maine in 1959? And why did Ellen live with their father in Derry, when Robert lived in Augusta with their mother? Why were two sons from my father's first marriage parceled out the same way? What elements of the day in Augusta enabled me to learn chess rapidly, play it with an idiot savant's expertise, and why couldn't I even tell how the pieces moved when I saw a chess set again? Why were we watching the Army-McCarthy Hearings on my grandmother's black-and-white Motorola in the daytime, in the spring of 1954? Why does a four-year-old retain, sixty years afterward, the mental picture of Roy Cohn whispering in Joe McCarthy's ear in the Senate hearing room? Was it Edward R. Murrow who advised "the viewing audience" to remove any children from the room, which they didn't, before showing ten-year-old footage of the extermination camps in Poland?

Winters: five, six, ten feet of snow on the ground until April, packed enough to carve out igloos and tunnels we rummaged in all day, unfazed by the cold. Summers: the raw geography on the edge of town, primordial forests, streams, meadows; places where miles of tarmac roll up and down pinewood hills, suddenly becoming level where a spooky row of pastel houses appears, occupied by people nobody knows anything about.

A dirt road near the Londonderry line ran straight through a forest like a tunnel of leaves, ending in a jungle of weeds and tangled vegetation. A lone frame-house and a wrecked Oldsmobile rusting on cinder blocks suddenly visible across a narrow gully. That became a drinking spot in high school, a road at the end of the world that vanished like everything else as the town got raped by developers.

The road started below an overpass of Interstate 93, some of which occupies a thousand acres the state of New

Hampshire expropriated from my family by eminent domain. My Aunt Jane ran her horses there. After the road went through she sold them, since there was nowhere left to ride. I had never noticed the road, which my family had probably owned in the sweet by-and-by, before the interstate made it hard to pick it out of the landscape. I discovered it while driving around with Joyce, an obese, slow-witted girl who owned a white Chevy convertible. She had flunked out of high school and drove aimlessly all day, or sat for hours parked in the lot behind St. Thomas Aquinas Church.

Joyce is obsessed with a young priest who lives in the rectory. She lusts after him with the grinning obtusity of a Macy's blimp on Thanksgiving, even claims they've "been together," though she often gives whatever did or more likely didn't happen a taint of molestation, hinting that this nondescript liturgical frock took advantage of a very special fat girl's piety and thirst for scriptural revelation. She's wet for this nobody in a Roman collar, but it's weirdly jumbled up with an obsessive fervor that springs, somehow, from obscure antagonisms in Joyce's family. She constructs a four-foot replica of the cathedral in Manchester out of wooden matchsticks.

Joyce gets sent to juvie after she breaks into the parish rectory and menaces the young Father Hannigan as well as the older priest in residence there. Whatever it was she actually did, it was bound to happen—Joyce is crazy for Jesus, or possibly just crazy. After being released from juvie she vanishes, briefly reappearing after several years to reveal that she's become a Franciscan nun. She even wears a wimple to prove it.

My black-and-white dog Lassie, whom Kev traps in a blanket and pushes down the stairs. The forbidding crawl space behind a little latched door in the kitchen of the old house. The equally strange crawl space created when my father doesn't finish the underside wall supporting the porch of the new house. Time stands still, as if the world has died a quiet death. Grampa's vegetable garden, his potting shed full of acrid-smelling fertilizer bags, wheelbarrow, spades, hoes, rakes, saws. Gramma's zinnias, petunias, white and purple lilac bushes. Mumma: It's their house, until we move it's their rules. Gramma adores my brother. Me she loathes, the saucy runt who shouldn't have happened. My mother isn't Kev's mother. Kev's mother, Flo, is in the Maine state asylum. Aunt Bettie: Flo tried to stab your father with scissors. Mumma: Flo came to visit once when they let her out for a while, you wanted her to take you back on the train with her. Uncle Buck: He likes a nut case better than he likes his uncle, what did you expect, spoiling him like that?

Whistle while you work, Stevenson's a jerk, Eisenhower's got the power, whistle while you work. Dealing blackjack at age seven in the V.F.W. Drunk Daddy: Gary has the gift. Look how he shoots those cards. Drunk Daddy is not a veteran of any foreign wars, only one interminable domestic one, but he's welcome there for his disreputable skill set. Drunk Daddy runs a floating poker game upstate on week nights and supervises a roulette wheel and a blackjack table at the Elks in Hooksett on the weekends. He won the lumber mill off Ben Adams in an all-night craps game a month before V-J Day, then sold half of it back, Drunk Daddy the Ever Generous and Taken Advantage Of. He drives a forklift, unloading the boxcars and hauling the lumber to a shed, and tallies the receipts during the day, sinking his winnings as well as his self-written paycheck back into the company, which sinks faster than he can bail it out.

This is what I learned from my father: how to drive a stick shift, how to saddle a skittish horse, the proper method of waxing skis, what to use for bait when deep-sea fishing, the humane way to kill a timber rattler with a shovel. Also how to win and lose a fortune in a blackjack game in less than thirty minutes. Uncle Buck: When's he gonna grow some hair on his chest so we can tell if he's a boy or a girl? Uncle Dilly: Pick on someone your own size, why don't you. Uncle Buck: If any of you was my own size, maybe I would. He knows I'm only teasing him, don't you, kid?

Mumma: You can go to Bettie's house after school and I'll come get you after work, you'd like that, wouldn't you? Gramma has pushed my mother too far and can't be trusted taking care of me. Gramma gives my belongings to Kev whenever he lies and claims something's his. He grabs whatever I treasure, even things he doesn't want, broken toys, old *TV Guides*, the bottle caps Bill Sharits, the old grouch at the store down on Crystal Avenue, lets me scoop out of the catcher bin under the opener on his soda cooler. I hate my grandmother, I tell my aunt. Bettie: Don't ever say you hate people, if your grammy died you'd be sorry. She hates me, so why shouldn't I? She doesn't hate you, she's an old lady set in her ways. She acts the same with you and Kev as she did with your father and your Uncle Eli, she picks one over the other. She never liked your father divorcing Flo. Flo was closer to her than your mother. Why would she like Flo over my mother? Because, your grandmother and Flo are Jewish. Does that mean I'm Jewish? You're a small fraction Jewish. (Years later I learn that none of this is true.) Your grandfather isn't Jewish, he belongs to the Knights of Pythias. What did she do to become Jewish? Why is Flo Jewish? If a person's Jewish, they descended from Jews, like the Bergerons are descended from Canada. But didn't they kill Jesus and spare Barabbas? Bettie: I don't know, was I there? Maybe they told the Romans to kill Jesus way back when that happened, but your grandmother didn't do it. She's not responsible for it, she's assimilated. Flo tried to kill my father, didn't she? That wasn't religious, she did that because Flo is insane. Anyway your father provoked her, is what I think. But don't go repeating that or your mother will blow a gasket.

Suez Crisis. The Russians invade Hungary with tanks. What if the Russians drop the hydrogen bomb, we're only sixty miles from Boston. Why do we all have to die on their say-so? They're not going to drop the goddamn bomb, will you stop worrying about it? The Russkies know they'd be wiped out before their missiles even got here. We'll all die when we're good and ready. Mumma runs for town clerk, a real political campaign. The car's full of thousands of offset photo reproductions of her face on rectangular cards with her name and Republican Party affiliation. She wins. Suddenly our grocery allowance doesn't depend on a hand Drunk Daddy holds in a poker game.

Miss Anderson's piano lessons. The veins in her scary shrink-wrap hands bulge like blue-purple worms. I haven't practiced and stare at the keyboard in a pubescent, semiconscious trance. It takes a lot for Miss Anderson to lose her patience. She has always been approvingly gentle; her anger now is gently expressed but unmistakable. You were such a good pupil for years, but now I have to wonder if you even want to learn this. Miss Anderson's handwriting is thin as silk thread, strands of delicate whorling penmanship, like Prince Myshkin's in *The Idiot*. Miss Anderson's mysteriously wealthy sister lives in a wedding-cake mansion on the hill above Miss Anderson's house, a dollhouse by comparison. No one besides the maid and Dr. Tietelbaum, who scrapes my ears in the winter, has glimpsed the other Miss Anderson in thirty-seven years.

Drunk Daddy notices me reading *Death in the Afternoon*, from his own Collier's complete edition of *The Works of Ernest Hemingway*. With the musing air of a shit-faced philosopher he says: Ya know, Hemingway flirted with Communism for a while. No, I tell him, trying to sound worldly and clued in about sex, he flirted with Marlene Dietrich. He *fucked* Marlene Dietrich, Drunk Daddy trumps, swigging his CC and ginger ale, he *flirted* with Communism. "Fuck" is the one word no one's allowed to say in our house, and I can tell he's drunker than I've ever seen him when he says it. I've already figured out that Mumma and Daddy never, ever fuck, that it's the reason he hates her, and hates himself, and his wanting to fuck is the reason she hates him, and hates herself. I don't know how I know this and I don't want to know it, I don't even know what fucking is but I somehow know it's what married people are supposed to do, and that they don't.

Sputnik. Why can't we build a bomb shelter in the new house? Daddy: Because the odds are, if there's a nuclear war, and we go running like ninnies to a bomb shelter, we'll bake to death slowly like a batch of Toll House cookies. Lousy way to go if you ask me.

School: If we donate twenty-five cents a week to Catholic Charities, we'll redeem one pagan baby in Red China by the end of the year, supporting our missionaries who are shown on the pamphlets the nuns hand out being martyred by Chinese Communists who drive long, rusty spikes into their skulls with what appear to be ordinary toolbox hammers. These agonizing deaths draw them even closer to the Sacred Heart of Jesus than they already were.

Bookcase in Aunt Bettie's parlor: *Act One* by Moss Hart, *The Interpretation of Dreams* by Sigmund Freud, *Forever Amber* by Kathleen Winsor, *How to Stop Worrying and Start Living* by Dale Carnegie, *Masters of Deceit* by J. Edgar Hoover, *None Dare Call It Treason* by John A. Stormer, *How to Be Free and Happy* by Bertrand Russell, *The Conquest of Happiness* by Bertrand Russell, *Why I Am Not a Christian* by Bertrand Russell, *Peyton Place* by Grace Metalious, *Witness* by Whittaker Chambers, *Jane Eyre* by Charlotte Brontë, *Peace of Soul* by Bishop Fulton J. Sheen, *Out of Bondage* by Elizabeth Bentley, *By Love Possessed* by James Gould Cozzens, *Ecstasy and Me* by Hedy Lamarr, *Exodus* by Leon Uris, *I Chose Freedom* by Victor Kravchenko, *100 More Jokes for the John*, the Bible, *How to Win at Canasta*.

Elvis Presley on the *The Ed Sullivan Show*. Ernie Kovacs. Edie Adams commercials for Muriel cigars. "A woman is only a woman, but a good cigar is a smoke." Milton Berle. Dean Martin, drinking. Judy Canova, singing. Sonja Henie, skating. *77 Sunset Strip*, tonight starring Efrem Zymbalist, Jr., and Edd "Kookie" Byrnes. "Kookie, Kookie, lend me your comb." Fabian. *I Love Lucy. Leave It to Beaver. Our Miss Brooks. I Remember Mama. The Many Loves of Dobie Gillis*, starring Bob Denver, and Tuesday Weld as Thalia Menninger. *O! Susanna* and *The Gale Storm Show* starring Gale Storm, featuring ZaSu Pitts. William Bendix in *The Life of Riley*. A test of the Emergency Broadcast System. Oscar Levant, Dody Goodman, Alexander King, Malcolm Muggeridge on *The Jack Paar Tonight Show*.

The new house, across the street from the old house. Shotgun in the hall closet. Drunk Daddy: One of these days I'm going to take that gun and put all of you out of your misery. Mumma: Your father doesn't mean what he's saying. Even if he did shoot me, he would never shoot you. Why do I have to have the same room as Kev? This house is so big, why can't I have my own room? Because, that's why. If your father ever finished that attic he could build you one. When Kev leaves for college you'll have the whole room to yourself. A medley of nuclear porn beside my bed: *Alas, Babylon*; *On the Beach*; *A Canticle for Leibowitz*; *Fail-Safe*; *Seven Days in May*; *Dr. Strangelove*. Beside Kev's bed: tennis racquets, tennis balls, ping-pong paddles, baseball glove, basketball, basketball trophy, football, football trophy, football helmet, varsity sweater, jock strap, gym sweats, chemistry book, physics book, *A Treasury of American Short Stories*, foil-wrapped rubbers pressed between the mattress and the box spring.

In the town, shoplifting from the paper store: *1984, Anna Karenina, Babbitt, The Jungle, Crime and Punishment, Lolita.* Signet paperbacks, cover illustrations by Milton Glaser.

A thirty-five-year-old music teacher at the high school who isn't from around here and was only teaching there this one semester is found face down in the Merrimack River. Somehow mutilated but no one says this, it's somehow understood from how people don't say it. There had been hushed adult talk about him from day one, nobody says the word "queer" either, when kids ask their parents about it they're told the music teacher "got mixed up with jazz musicians."

Sunday morning at the Family Drug fountain: Mayde Giblin and her companion Emmi. Mayde a world-weary retired nurse, stout and imperishable-looking in an apple-green car coat. Emmi, belted in the gray raincoat worn by spies, sickly and thin. And German, like Rosa Klebb in

From Russia, with Love. Blanchie Ceviskas overhears
everything and stares through thick glasses making her
eyes huge and goofy looking, thinking up something funny
to say so someone will talk to her. She lets her bedridden
mother, who's ninety-one, believe she's at Mass, praying
for the old bag's soul to rise into Heaven right off the bat
when the time comes, without doing any time in Purgatory.
Blanchie drinks cup after acrid cup of coffee in the Family
Drug instead. People cluck pityingly that she never managed
to find a husband, but I happen to know she was never
looking for one, though I don't know how I know it. Neither
was Mayde Giblin, who I sense is Emmi's wife, though
that's vague. Blanchie Ceviskas is smarter than people
realize. She knows what secretly goes on in our town. She's
not a gossip, but people don't fool her. She knows when
she's being patronized, too, but she's too dignified to say
so. Mayde Giblin has opinions about the town as well:
petty, ignorant, bigoted, and pathetic, full of shits trying
to pass themselves off as gold.

Mayde's house is on 28, near Chanticleer Motel Lounge,
popular with married people cheating on each other when
it first opened but now nobody goes there. Mayde's first
floor has no furniture, other than a scarred mahogany
dining table with chairs around it. A pile of *Fact* magazines
stops open the kitchen door. The topmost, black-and-
white cover: "Who Killed Dag Hammarskjöld?"

Bobby Giblin hobbles down from his upstairs on his
clubfoot. Bobby Giblin is a painter. He gives me drawing
lessons, and shows me how to mix colors. He paints on
sheets of a coated paper I am never able to locate anywhere
in years to come, even in Boston. It's nearly as thin as
ordinary paper, but, chemically laminated, it doesn't buckle
or break apart no matter how much oil it absorbs.

I incessantly hope a different, better family will adopt
me. I'm happier around Mayde, Emmi, and Bobby than I
ever am at home. After I've known them a few months,
during one of Mumma's interminable nightly recitations
of every single tedious thing that happened all day at her
office, she remarks as if it's nothing important that Mayde
Giblin dropped dead that afternoon, news I don't react to
at all, even when Mumma, oblivious, says, "You knew Mayde
Giblin, didn't you?" Because I have kept my feelings about
anything barricaded against Mumma and Drunk Daddy
for years. They tell me how to dress and how to eat and
how to act and how to talk and what friends I can have and
which relatives I should care about and which ones think
their shit doesn't stink because they moved to Connecticut
and who in the town I should look down my nose at and
who to steer clear of, who is good and who is trash and
what college I will go to and what I should do with my life
if I don't want to wind up poor like they both were in the
Depression and all through the war and if I ever told them
I really, really loved anything besides them they would run
right over it until it was roadkill.

After Mayde dies, Bobby disappears. Nobody ever sees
Emmi in the town again, either. Mumma takes us all to a
convention at The Balsams two or three years later. As
Drunk Daddy, Aunt Pam, and Bettie pillage a buffet, Ellen
and I wander off into the red-carpeted halls of the vast
resort hotel and somehow lose our way in a basement, a
maze of corridors with massive steam pipes hissing under
low ceilings. It's completely deserted, except for a dining
room waiter we suddenly spot opening a door at the far
end of a long hallway.

Surprise, it's Bobby Giblin. My happiness at seeing
him makes me realize that I loved him, all that time he

lived in Derry. I'm old enough now to recognize sexual attraction. That I want him to kiss me, lie down on top of me in bed. I want this impossible thing, in the basement of the hotel. When our eyes meet, my skin tingles. I can't really tell, but I want to believe he wants to be alone with me, that something would happen, we would "make love" in some way, if we were alone. He asks Ellen how long we're all staying, then invites us into the room.

The hotel manager gave him an empty storage space to use as a studio, he says: the manager likes his paintings. Bobby's working in the dining room all summer. The room has paintings and art stuff all over, also a sleeping cot and a refrigerator. Bobby's really only talking to me—Ellen sees that he's my friend, that we have things to say to each other that don't include her. She's the only relative I have who treats me as a person, instead of a child to boss around.

The Balsams is lucky to get one-third occupancy during the one season they open. It was posh in the Roosevelt era but it's a third-choice convention center now. I want to ask Bobby why he's living up north, it's such an unpopulated wasteland. Why he disappeared right after Mayde died. I know why, though: Derry is a shithole, they all would've moved on by this time if Mayde were still alive, anyway.

He shows us his paintings, which are intense, frightening, too graphically suggestive of clawed-open flesh and morbidity for Ellen to give them more than polite looks. She's squeamish. But she tells Bobby in a really nice way that she's never had the opportunity to learn anything about art, and wishes she did know enough to appreciate it. She means it, too.

I want to see Bobby again while this convention lasts. He can tell me how I can be an artist and how I can get far away from New Hampshire and my family and survive in the world. Maybe he'll kiss me, hold me, make me feel loved. He'll rub his penis against me, or something. But my family is actually having fun for a change without turning vile after several hours, and I forget to look for him again until the night before we leave, and then I can't find him. Ellen, later: I wonder how Bobby Giblin can wait on tables in that huge place, with a foot like that?

None of us leaves town except in a family bubble, so when we go anywhere, the town comes with us. In town, each family is its own sealed-off country, surrounded by other countries they don't trust. Ever since my father bought the lot he built our house on from Phil Bartlett, we've been in a silent war against the Bartletts, concerning the property markers. My parents believe Phil Bartlett surreptitiously shifts them at night when he thinks he can get away with it, stealing another inch or two of land each time. Mrs. Bartlett is Parisian and thinks she's better than us, because Mumma speaks Canuck French, and forgets a lot of the language. Plus, Phil Bartlett feels superior because he's a licensed surveyor.

They're neutral about the Dumonts one street over, as the Dumonts are the parents of my mother's friend Leona Deroscher, who's married to Leo Deroscher, Drunk Daddy's best Drunk Friend. Leona divorces Leo, goes into AA, and sensibly grows distant from my parents.

Crush on Kev's friend Eugene Barbosa. Mumma says he's trash. The Barbosas are guineas who live in Pinardville, a place always mentioned with disdain and dread. Pinardville begins after the last utility pole of Cityville. I have never really understood how these two places are differentiated, since they seem to occupy exactly the same area. Ben Adams lives in Pinardville, the less desirable of the two, and he's rich. Amelia Adams has leukemia, always fatal.

Mumma drags me to her bedside. A fan is blowing in the window. Won't she catch cold from that fan? Mumma: She doesn't want us to smell the cancer.

I write down clumsy, clueless fantasies of putting Eugene Barbosa's penis in my mouth. It's said to be huge as a donkey's, it's a joke among my brother's friends. I record this in a composition notebook with a marbled white-and-black cover that I swiped from the paper store. It doesn't occur to me to hide the notebook. Notebooks are private, like diaries. Mumma finds it in my room and immediately reads it. It's a revelation of sorts that she has no concept of privacy at all where I'm concerned. Worse, she now believes I really sucked Eugene Barbosa, whose sister and I drove her Falcon on a recent wild-goose chase, upstate around Cornish, hoping to find J. D. Salinger's house. Nothing I say dissuades Mumma from her dirty certainty that I've been molested by some filthy Portuguese delinquent. Since nothing sexual can ever be spoken in our family, aside from lame jokes the adults cackle over when they're loaded, she doesn't know what she can do about it, and finally, grudgingly, realizes she can't do anything. At first, though, I'm afraid she'll call up Eugene, who'll hate me forever, or say something to his parents, even though they're trash who would naturally have no control of their kids.

I glean that she thinks I'm naturally ashamed of my desires—and that Mumma believes, or wants to believe, that an evil outside influence infected me with a disease only psychiatry can now cure. But at this juncture in the family's fortunes, psychiatry is still unmanageably expensive, so she reads up on the subject in the popular literature, and decides to believe "sensitive" boys afflicted with tendencies outgrow them after adolescence.

I'm not ashamed, but definitely embarrassed, and not entirely for myself; it wasn't a believably written fantasy, and Mumma's credulity makes her seem stupid, as well as damningly prepared to think "the worst," as she conceives it, about this child she's molded in her image as much as she possibly could, with a certain palpable if unconscious resentment. This is the first sad instance of our nurturing bond mutating into something unbearably oppressive and heartbreaking. In time it becomes a wretched spell I try to shatter by putting myself in extreme situations that would give her a heart attack if she knew about them. To break free of her personal force field, it finally becomes necessary to put the entire continent between us.

Hot-walking saddlebreds at Rockingham. When can I race? Not this year. When? Next summer we'll put you in the starting race, right when the track opens, and see how you do. Paregoric cigarettes, smoked on my bed with a faunlike boy I worship, who works busing trays in the track cafeteria. We make out a little but it scares him, and I'm afraid we'll get caught.

First blowjob: Paul Carlisle. His skin's dark for a Caucasian but his family's considered white. He has the biggest hard-on of any boy at St. Thomas Aquinas School, it's well known. I suck him off all through seventh grade. We have nothing in common, but what more do you really need in common in the seventh grade? We hook up again in eighth grade, not as many times, and five or six times in high school. Years after I leave town, when I return to visit I run into Paul now and then in places like the A&P parking lot. He's married by that time, to Fayanne Parker, the daughter of my mother's friend Gerrie Trobick by her first husband. We talk about old times, prolong the conversation in his car, or my car. Invariably, I give him another blowjob.

Terpin hydrate and codeine cough syrup, obtainable without prescription at Family Drug. Crush on Seth Willard, a geekily beautiful senior who's nice to me, which most older boys aren't. After classes he's the school janitor. He lets me tag along on his job, through the hallowed, gothic crumb cake where none of us is getting more than a modicum of education. Stoned on codeine, I not-very-secretly adore his back, his ass, his arms, his legs, his hands, his feet, his pale, smooth skin as he mops from the top floor to the main hall, which is lined with mementos of totally forgotten human beings who suffered four years of strangulating boredom in this very building.

Seth's sister Heidi dates the most thrillingly formed boy at Pinkerton Academy, Donny Samara. He's considered impossibly gorgeous and sexy by the girls in school. His father owns Weeping Willow Trailer Park on Route 3. Heidi Willard is decent, so he's never put it to her, he confides one day. But even making out with Donny Samara, I imagine, feeling his pink, wet tongue in your mouth, must set off multiple orgasms. I idolize him in a creepy pathetic way, and make bad drawings of his face from memory that I give him proudly as if they're by Leonardo. I hang around where he parks his truck in town on his trailer park errands, for the slight chance of talking to him and looking at him for two minutes. It's not exactly a friendship. I'm more his fan club. I'm too naïve to understand that he sees I'm in love with him, or that it's public knowledge at school. Paul Carlisle still asks for a blowjob now and then, I never say no. Whenever I lap his balls, I close my eyes and pretend they're Donny's.

Second blowjob: Donny Samara, his lanky frame arranging itself in a tense sprawl behind the wheel of a blue Corvair his father bought him for his seventeenth birthday. "Norwegian Wood," a Beatles tune that's supposedly a coded song about smoking marijuana, plays on the car radio. We drink Bacardi from a bluish-green quart bottle. An unbearably long pretense that we're only out drinking together causes both of us to become sloppy drunk before Donny dares to unzip his fly and unbelt his denim slacks, pushing them and his white briefs down far enough to expose his stiffy and balls to my trembling lips. It's too dark to see them, but that's no obstacle to what we both knew was going to happen before we started drinking. Donny pushes my head down gingerly and slides his organ into my mouth, which he pumps in a clinically measured way, as if he's anxious to do it correctly. I vomit all over his crotch.

The Kelley brothers who take turns frenching me at the Pine Island fair, aping the male star of some romance film they saw on television. I win an ugly lamp throwing darts at a wall of balloons. A baby comes out of Bella Talbot's vagina that she didn't even know was inside her, in the girl's bathroom at lunch hour. Bettie tells Ellen in her throaty, hectoring voice that a woman can get pregnant from using the same water a man took a bath in. Klev-Bro Shoe fire burns down Uncle Babe's store, turning three blocks of Railroad Avenue into smoldering cinders along with it. It's widely debated that a woman whose charred remains are found on a sled in the Manchester woods may not be the third victim of the local serial killer, but a case of spontaneous combustion. Mumma falls off a gelding and gets right back up in the saddle though she's scared to death, because that's how we do. Daddy burns the entire epidermis off his right arm cooking fried dough "blubbies" in a cauldron of boiling oil. They sew his fingers into his stomach temporarily to grow the skin back.

Third blowjob: Richard Wacker, really his name, whose
parents operate a bungalow-type motor inn in Salem that
I drive past all the time while I'm training at Rockingham.
The bungalows ring a kidney-shaped pond and suggest a
magnified miniature-golf course. This is the year my bones
grow too big for me to stay at the requisite jockey weight,
and the thoroughbred owner who offered to sponsor me
says if he tries to enter me in a race I'll get disqualified.
Richard Wacker's glistening teeth, his dark feathery hair.
His fleshy lips. His lascivious mouth. Richard Wacker is
my image of perfection for at least a year. No one else is
interested in him that way because he's exotic, ethnic in
some indefinable disturbing manner, and the expressions
on his face point to an indecently wide and precocious
range of sexual experience. After unbuttoning his corduroys
he pushes my face into his kissing-fresh underpants,
moaning joyously when the head of his cock presses into
my mouth. He instantly spurts out a little splash of semen,
which I swallow to show how much I really care for him.
After a stunned moment Richard Wacker asks, in a drowsy,
sweetly earnest voice, if his dick is bigger than Donny
Samara's.

Last month I went to the zoo in Edinburgh to visit the penguins. The day was so blowy the treetops thrashed in the wind with a shirring sound like crashing surf. Finally rain thin as needles fell and the zoo closed the park. I only had time to see the giant sloths and pink flamingos and a leathery aquatic mammal I don't know the name of moving swiftly back and forth under the inky water of his pond. The penguins were diving and feeding, feeding and diving. The zookeepers, in yellow smocks and blue galoshes, hand-fed them whole, dead fish. They snapped the fish up as if pulling them from a vending machine. We love penguins, but that is one-sided. No penguins will talk to you. No penguins will even look at you unless you are close enough to be a threat. Why should they? Unless you are holding a dead fish, no penguin has any reason to go near you. That is the way of penguins, and it always will be.

two

In the morning before Neyda arrives from where she lives with her husband in a housing block behind the Melia Cohiba Hotel, I sharpen pencils and write in notebooks for an hour or two. One day, when I'm dead, dozens if not hundreds of notebooks of every conceivable quality and kind will be found, some covered front to back with drafts of novels, drafts of stories, drafts of essays, occasional poems and what have you, but most will contain a formless jumble of stray thoughts, phone numbers, addresses, names, quotations, lists, coded messages, and Internet passwords, among other things, in a schizoid variety of scrawls, letter sizes, and penmanship styles, often occupying only a few pages of an otherwise blank volume:

Item No. 46012
Norcom, Inc.
Griffin, GA 30224
www.norcominc.com
Made in Brazil

Napoleon only liked to spend 15–20 minutes on dinner pour le bonne table, Mme Recamier et al 'Almanach des Gourmands' (1803–12) (beat gigot until tender) British blocade 1812 shortage of ingredients: no rum, coffee, chocolate or sugar coming from French W Indies

ATTN: Debby Wilbur
    Send form
                    $1000.00
                    March 1
~~Miami rentals~~
~~Camera battery~~
~~Call car service~~
        (Cuban oceanic research
        biodiversity sphere)

Fouché – 'bad style of company—muddy boots,
    doubtful linen'
Bank crash of 1805
No dining room @ Tuileries, would lay table in
different room every day

Flight record locator XTTQOF

        *Anaconda – 11", 5'11", $260 – 816-877-1589
        Miguel 559-519-7988 'always safe' 5'10" big
        getinurazz1 (raw freak) 6'2", 9" 678-457-5037
        *Jeffi 6'2", 10", 150/hr 305-514-0565

transfer pictures to flash drive

    N ate fast, ate everything, but liked good wines—
Chambertin, Clos-Vougeot, Château Lafite
    Juliette Récamier – Chateaubriand
    "led on" Lucien Bonaparte & rejected him (covered
    walls with
        mirrors)

her party on Dec 16 1804 — snarled up 6,000
coaches in traffic

Psalms 115:6 -- *aures habent et non audient*

Royalist rebellions in the Vendée during French Revolution

to give you the general effect. I brought a pile of "used" notebooks with me, along with ones yet unmarked, and I'll probably find some use for what I've already written in them, because if you note things as chaotically as I do, eventually you find that you've already written down, months or years earlier, any "new" idea that comes into your mind: on the whole, a deflating discovery. One wants to flush everything out, become a geyser of originality, but *no hay posibilidad de esto en absoluto.* I am often ridiculous enough to imagine I can pursue several projects simultaneously—something experience has repeatedly disproven—and therefore need a separate notebook for each one.

At least I am here, again, finally, away from the electronic mental gunk of Very Late Capitalism, US style, which I'm convinced will soon drive everyone who isn't already a zombie over the edge.

When New York ruins my day, I think about this terrace. I imagine myself sitting here, at this round glass table that easily seats twelve (I'm not sure we have that many chairs in the flat, but I could borrow some from a neighbor). I picture the zebra plants and majesty palms in terra cotta tubs that line the terrace. I visualize Neyda rolling the grimy red-and-white awning with the hand crank dangling from the awning brace. Or unrolling it when the sun's blazing. I hear the elevator thubbing to a stop at this floor, the cheap plastic telephone's faint, infrequent ring. This is my favorite place in the house, whether I'm writing or not.

Señora Carlotta Dominguez is at last in residence next door. I have been missing her, because that empty apartment spooks me a little when I get off the elevator at night. Sometimes the hall light is off because I forget nobody's next door to switch it on after dark. Alberto was over there for three days relinquishing his own flat after I arrived, but then he went back to Bogotá.

Señora Carlotta Dominguez is a tiny, avid vamp of sixty-eight who looks like an Andalusian grandmother, which she is, and Alberto's maternal aunt. She has an ardent lover a third her age who comes in from Matanzas to see her, and two others repining for her in other countries. When I saw the Cuban lover on her terrace back in January, I couldn't look at him and breathe at the same time. This proves there should always be hope.

Carlotta arrived last night on the Madrid flight, gleeful, cackling at her own fun while the taxi driver unloaded her luggage on the sidewalk. I was on my terrace, smoking and

drinking rum colas in the dark with Brayon Lazaro Silva
from Artemisa province. Brayon Lazaro Silva had sent me
a note via cocktail waitress in Las Vegas Club a week ago.
The message was so funny and blunt I had to spend the
night with him. We got very drunk first. We got very drunk
again last night. Señora Carlotta Dominguez was in such
an effervescent mood that she came over and got drunk
with us.

Carlotta is peering over the edge of her terrace as I
write this, smiling at passing birds, the trees, the clouds.
She casts a pointed glance down at voices rising from the
entrada, shaking her dyed onyx curls. She waves at me
and cocks an ear at a burst of laughter below. Often we
communicate by making faces. Her expression says that
the workers swarming in and out are predictably taking
their sweet time with the repairs, it's obvious at a glance,
but it's not unpleasant having them around, it makes a
change, so why be bothered? We both remember the elevator
going out for a month after the rains last spring; the dilatory
cosmetic work underway is comparatively painless. Neither
of us enjoyed climbing the back stairs, the lights in the
stairwell short out all the time, and for her it was a real
physical ordeal.

If I am not mistaken, two house painters are currently
planted on the stoop and plan on dawdling there until the
rest of their crew arrives. Which could be anytime between
now and next Tuesday. It's a state job. They're paid whether
they show up for it or not. The painters claim to be making
their methodical way up here, a floor at a time, though in
reality they work on any floor they can loiter on, where
the tenants are gone for the day. It's wise to keep an eye
on them when they're in your apartment. Nobody cares if
they slack off, but they might pilfer something if given

the opportunity.

They're repainting terrace ceilings and other surfaces damaged in last month's four-week deluge. They're also giving the stairwell, terra incognita since the elevator got repaired, a fresh coat, and have turned that into festive picnic grounds. One of the painters has his eye on me. A few days ago he tapped at the back door and asked Neyda for a cup of coffee. I focused his fuzzy form across the salon once he stepped inside, furtively checking him out while he stood in the kitchen drinking it. Down here, fascination with male beauty impedes my progress. I continually remind myself it's irrelevant to what I'm trying to do.

When attractive men show up at the door on their own initiative, though, I become the prone cataleptic in *I Walked with a Zombie*. There's no disputing it's a role I was born to play. While the painter sipped his coffee, slouched against the utility closet, shirtless, paint speckled, looking remote, I sensed he was taking his sweet time with his coffee break, too. Unexpectedly, he shot me a swift, scorchingly direct look. It was like noticing a sniper on a distant rooftop a second late. Then he averted his face and handed Neyda the empty mug, wiped his hands on his spattered jeans, and left.

Now he nods and half-smirks for a second when I pass him in the building, as if we share a secret. It's hardly a secret, since his coworkers all catch these utterly casual signals and totally get what they signify, and couldn't care less about it. Cuban men will screw a grapefruit if there's nothing else around. Their need to fuck as much as possible is a given. Who they do it with isn't even considered a worthwhile topic of gossip unless it's a case of incest. He's handsome, no question. Full crown of black ringlets, moistly ponderous, anthracitic eyes, lips from the African heart of Baracoa, is my best guess. He never wears a shirt so I see how well he's put together on a daily basis.

It was no surprise to me that this man knew he was going to fuck me the instant we made eye contact. I knew it, he knew it, go know. Despite the languid pace of everything else here, nobody wastes any time or breath establishing this silent understanding. It's effortless. He's not in any hurry about it. I'm not either. At the rate they're going, he'll be around at least another month.

★

Things to remember better: Ferd Eggan entered my life in San Francisco in 1969. I had dropped out of Berkeley. I had what today are called sexual identity issues that made it impossible to focus in any degree-winning manner on philosophy and English literature, my purported areas of study. I had drifted away from classes and moved out of student housing, crashing at various communes around the Berkeley campus. One was a Trotskyite commune. Another housed a study group of Frankfurt School scholars with guest lectures by Herbert Marcuse and also raised money for the Tupamaros. Another went in for encounter sessions and scream therapy. My final Berkeley commune was devoted to growing peyote cacti and magic mushrooms. I met Ferd on a film set. He was helming a new wrinkle in the developing canon of narrative porn cinema from his own co-authored script, *The Straight Banana* ("exhibitionist flashes nymphomaniac, fucking ensues!"—a meet-cute picture). I was "sexually involved" by that time—not on camera—with one of the stars of *The Straight Banana*, a tall, bisexual Nebraskan refugee often billed as Mr. Johnny

Raw, or plain Johnny Raw, whose penis was a minor celebrity in the Bay Area.

Johnny Raw, aka Leonard Jones of Omaha, lived in the Marina district. I never socialized with him. I hardly knew him. I didn't care about him. His self-involvement was hermetic and vaguely reptilian. Johnny Raw referred to the creeps who bought tickets to jerk off watching his films as "the fans," and believed he was an actual movie star. He was boastful, stupid, pathetically narcissistic, and sad, but such a deluded asshole it was impossible to feel sorry for him. I liked how he looked, he liked how I looked looking at him, that was literally all we shared. Whenever we stumbled over each other that summer, both in half-drunk stupors, in the same bar, at the same midnight hour, we rushed robotically to the Marina in a cab, and got it on—without passing Go, without collecting two hundred dollars, without spending a minute longer in each other's company afterward than I needed to put my clothes on.

I never took my clothes off, actually. Johnny Raw usually pulled his dick and balls out of his fly or lowered his pants to his ankles. Gay youth today may find it incomprehensible, but "having sex" with Johnny Raw ten or fifteen times that summer didn't involve Johnny Raw fucking me, or me fucking Johnny Raw. I was unusually innocent for my age—and, it's the truth, unusually pretty and sought after at nineteen. I admit that by my present lights, I'd have to agree with former President Clinton that he "did not have sex with that woman." By today's standards, I had been around too long to hook up with men and then do nothing besides service them with a blowjob. But that's as far as I'd ever gone. Regardless of a precocious history of fellatio with other boys since the seventh grade, I had no concept of anal sex. I wasn't aware of it as something many people did. A true son of 1950s backwoods New Hampshire, I thought sodomy was an arcane, specialized perversion, like bestiality. Believed, in fact, that a rectum capable of accommodating even an average penis was such an aberration of nature that only rare, anally deformed individuals even attempted it. "Fucking," in my mind, meant male-on-female vaginal penetration.

For a while post-Berkeley, I lived in the attic of a hippie commune with no special theme going on, in a leased house on Seventeenth Street. By coincidence, a tenant below was Johnny Raw's costar in *The Straight Banana*. Grinda Pupic, a licensed practical nurse whose legal name was Bonnie Solomon, secured the attic for me when I moved across the bay, as a favor to a Berkeley friend of a friend.

A relentlessly sultry, ebulliently secular Jew, Bonnie's sangfroid enabled her to resume her side of an argument about local zoning laws between takes, while the bone-hard penis of a costar remained planted in her lady parts. Among friends and coworkers she exuded a generally misleading maternal solicitude. At the Nocturnal Dream Shows in North Beach, Bonnie sang with the Nickelettes, a hallucinatory, feminist auxiliary of the Cockettes. We occasionally had sex. I wasn't a frontal virgin. Bonnie was awfully nice and surprisingly tough.

I tagged along on a location shoot in the Sausalito hills, riding shotgun in a pickup driven by a hippie sound engineer, a roguishly bearded ex-Mouseketeer with a doomed aura named Brando Batty. (According to the state of California, that really was his real name. He once showed me his driver's license.) By nightfall I had a temp job, as emergency gaffer and continuity girl on *The Straight Banana* shoot. My thing with the eponymous Straight Banana (we just referred to him as Banana, really) quickly lapsed, in the easy manner of the day, into a different thing with Ferd, who already had a male squeeze and a more involved relationship with an older woman named Carol.

She wasn't much older, chronologically, but her weariness suggested she'd survived the *Titanic* and much else of cosmic historical significance. Older than a thousand years, still bitter over some deal gone terribly south in ancient Babylon, Carol sat stiffly in Brando Batty's truck all afternoon, penciling irritable remarks on the script she'd co-written, or flipping through *Variety*. I sensed a crazy attraction to Ferd, but became completely spellbound by Carol. She had the vibe of somebody who'd lived the nightmare in a big, expensive way. Short, wiry limbed, her glossy auburn hair poodled in a perky cut, she seemed implacable enough to launch a military coup in South America.

Sporadically emerging from her four-wheel bunker during lulls in the filming, she'd march directly up to Ferd to give him notes before talking to anyone else. She blinked theatrically at the sun; slid her sunglasses down from their nest in her hair; aimed a studied yawn in our general direction; lit a Marlboro with a silver lighter; smoothed her throat with the fingers she'd covered the yawn with. Each movement set off baffling signals, her private-looking little actions both seductive and off-putting, a selfishly generous display: as she studied her effect on people, Carol also telegraphed her utter indifference to whatever effect that was. I instinctively sensed she would shove me or anybody else out of a lifeboat if she thought they added too much weight. But I often dismissed as paranoid intuitions that were as obvious as giant letters on a billboard. Ferd was as easygoing as Carol was brittle. He japed, mugged, giggled, flirted, bantered with everyone while setting up shots, giving actors notes, squinting into the Arriflex viewfinder. His infectious looseness visibly stiffened when Carol asserted her presence. Their gravity together engraved a "serious" grown-up circle around them. The pornographic circus it excluded looked embarrassingly silly and juvenile, suddenly.

Which it was, of course. With the exception of Johnny Raw, however, we all saw the absurdity of a bunch of hippies making a porn movie. (Johnny Raw went on to fatuous national fame as the straight industry's favorite penis, with a best-selling dildo, molded from his cock, named after him—"get that Johnny Raw sensation at home." Johnny Raw bought the big sleep on a smack overdose at thirty, without a dime left. If you count in porn years, he had a long run.) They—we—were making trash to support ourselves at something we could bear waking up for. We had no delusions of glamour, though getting paid for anything at the time had a definite cachet. The stars were fucking people they would have fucked anyway, and sex for all involved (except me) was about as overheated as a sneeze. During Ferd and Carol's script conferences, they leaned against a white LeSabre convertible with bright red upholstery, where the film action was occurring in the back seat. The naked stars sat up looking dazed, smoked cigarettes, took bites from sandwiches. Cool breezes fluttered through the heat. We were on a dirt road high on a small mountain, a dreamy elevation with an awesome view of the bay.

To say I fell in love with Ferd the day I met him wouldn't be completely wrong, but sounds schmaltzy if I consider how little feeling I had for Johnny Raw from the jump, aside from a fascination with the body part that made him famous. In less than an hour around Ferd, Johnny evaporated from my consciousness.

Ferd was the first male I ever felt attracted to who was smarter than me, intellect never having been conspicuous in the few men I had "dated" before. Decades later, after his looks went, his charisma continued to make him beautiful, in a wasted, Egon Schiele way. I've thought about Ferd over much of my life, and find him full of contradictions, but this is what

seems constant: his intellectual finesse; his formidable conviction that his sense of reality trumped all others'; a decency
of heart often wildly at odds with situations I found him in, as
well as with the first two qualities I mentioned.

None of this was entirely apparent when I met him, when
he lived with Carol. I quickly got tangled up with both of them,
cast in confusing roles as an understudy to Ferd's boyfriend,
Chip (who I never knew beyond hello good-bye), and as a way-
ward urchin Ferd and Carol adopted. They collected people
like pollen sticking to their clothes: runaways, burnouts, lost
souls of all sorts. Carol acted as a vulpine den mother to a
shifting cast of acolytes and hangers-on.

She reigned over the upper floors of a five-story Victorian
on Broderick Street that exuded lifeless desuetude. Charles,
the owner, retired from some clandestine profession, occupied
in perpetuity a wing chair facing the fireplace in a musty floor-
through salon on the ground floor. He passed his days draining
tall cans of Rainier Ale while staring at a TV that was seldom
actually on, stacking ale cans in green pyramids that almost
brushed the high ceiling. Exactly where in that somnolent
house Charles kept the box of earth where he slept, I never
knew. His alleged college roommate, Steve, a more tangible,
slightly corpulent man of sixty-two, was given to "sporty" plaid
shirts, fishing pants with many pockets, and muted red loafers.
Steve inhabited a room in the basement. Charles was a man of
no words. Steve had a certain voluble *joie de vivre*. In a pinch,
one might call him jolly. He wasn't really.

In the fullness of time I became a tenant. I was given a
claustrophobic child-size room on the third floor containing
a canopied bed, a framed charcoal drawing of Leopold Sto-
kowski, and a ceiling bulb. But not yet.

Carol: eyes habitually narrow with suspicion, picking
over the ever-shifting assortment of Ferd's shag-mates and

"models" (as porn actors were then called), a poultry inspector in a battery farm. She spoke in rapid bursts, in tones of insulted intelligence. She was manic-depressive in a rapidly alternating, terrifying way. As Hoover Dam generates electricity, Carol generated fright and insecurity. She had been a girlfriend of Lenny Bruce. Or not. I later suspected that Carol inflated and embellished brushes with the well-known, to indicate that she was only briefly, disappointedly slumming among less exalted individuals for dark reasons known only to her. In retrospect, it's touching that the names Carol dropped were never household gods of celebrity culture ordinary people would recognize, but figures of the avant-garde: Jack Smith, Andy Warhol, Kenneth Anger, Gregory Markopoulos. (Looking back, I first heard of Werner Schroeter from Carol.) With these rarefied souls, Carol shared an understanding of Art's alchemical ways, its torturous difficulties, its isolating asceticism, communing with them in a spiritual Atlantis beyond our reach.

She lived off royalties from lyrics she'd written to a popular instrumental song that had played continuously on drive-time radio in California ever since 1963. Deep in her thirties, she evoked a rueful queen deposed from richer, more soigné and consequential realms. Spectral traces of an abandoned life entered the picture from time to time, in the form of a Paramount executive named Richard C——, who beamed in occasionally from Los Angeles, all Savile Row and attaché case, intent on rekindling a long-ago liaison in order to "bring Carol to her senses." Now and then, a reedy albino tax lawyer showed up with bales of papers for Carol to sign.

The autumn of 1969 was a creepy season in San Francisco. In the long, rancid afterglow of the summer of love, the Haight-Ashbury had puddled into a gritty slum of boarded-up head shops and strung-out junkies, thuggish dealers, undercover cops in love beads and fright wigs. The hippie saturnalia had continued as a sinister Halloween parody of itself, featuring overdoses and rip-offs and sudden flashes of violence.

I had long stringy hair the color of rusty tap water. I mostly wore shoplifted drag from thrift stores, "sensible" drag like pleated skirts and silk blouses. I looked androgynous enough to pass for a girl, unless I carried my Pan Am bag. (Flight bags were widely recognized as a fag accessory.) I was too reticent and unimposing to be a drag queen. I looked more like a flat-chested insurance secretary on a lunch break. But pretty— everyone said so. Lawrence Ferlinghetti picked me up one day in the park in North Beach. When catcalls from sunbathers who knew my actual gender alerted him to his mistake, he did the gentlemanly thing and took me to a café for a cup of coffee and made small talk.

Ferd shot smack more as a fashion statement than to quell an actual addiction. His personality was too controlling for him to enjoy the passivity of a heroin addict. Psychedelic drugs were taken like aspirin in San Francisco and heroin users were seen as the truly daring souls, more "seriously" troubled than aimless run-of-the-mill LSD dropouts. Ferd and Brando Batty, his partner in pseudo-addiction, sent me on missions to local emergency rooms to cop syringes. Ferd insisted that I go in drag, to what advantage I can't recall. At the hospitals I confessed my lack of insurance coverage, got parked in an examining room, stuffed a handful of needles in my flight bag before the doctor arrived, then sneaked away, never to be seen again. It worked every time.

I lived on no money, with no fixed address, becoming a ward of whatever boyfriend or commune whose orbit I drifted into. For a while I lived with one of Ferd's other smackmates, a torpid, troubled, horse-faced woman named Mary Blakey, aka Hamburger Mary, who usually came along on a nightly caravan to clubs and events with Ferd, Carol, Brando, and me, which sometimes included Ferd's other boyfriend, Chip. Mary hoarded drugs and secretly shot much more smack than Ferd did. She had a more developed habit, though neither of them was a junkie in the full-blown "I'll do anything for a fix" sense.

Mary never seemed fully conscious. She inhabited a private world where life's volume had been lowered to half decibel, like the darkened bedroom of a chronic migraine sufferer. The banished daughter of a Marin County ear, nose, and throat specialist, she had played Ferd's sister in a hard-core incest film with arty ambitions, *Billy Rainey's Brother*, and kept the model file for Lowell Pickett, Ferd's producer, up to date. For a month or so I slept in the Hollywood closet of her apartment on Leavenworth, while she "dated" a paroled gangster. We considered it the ultimate chic to consort with a genuine underworld type. Lionel was svelte and Italian and sexy, and really did have an air of danger about him, though who he really was we never learned. We plotted a bank robbery with him, an intricate scheme worthy of a bad screenplay that never advanced past the outline. I couldn't say now if we were serious or not. It was never clear at the time. We were desperate for something real to happen that would have consequences outside our little deer park. In any case, we all discussed the great plan so often and freely on the phone, between Leavenworth and Broderick Streets, that Lionel decided we were amateurs who would get arrested *entering* a bank. He tired of paying for Mary's heroin, and disappeared.

We went everywhere in a posse, collecting rootless, powerfully attractive, emotionally flattened hippies of both sexes, who were soon employed on the psychedelic fringe of the porn business, which orbited around the Sutter Theater in the Tenderloin.

Local impresarios were shedding their squarish image, personified in the elephantine tits and corny floor show of burlesque queen Carol Doda in North Beach, by showcasing flower children and generally pandering to the waning hippie movement, hoping to capture a nonexistent youth market. Since the films held little interest for this target demographic (why watch other people fuck when you can easily do it, and probably them, yourself?), the porn theaters threw LSD parties and gala premieres that filled up with local celebrities and stoned kids from the Castro. Janis Joplin, all boas and bangles, turned up at one gala where my erstwhile porn boyfriend screwed an actress on an elevated duvet in the lobby, while Les Nickelettes performed their version of "Deep in the Heart of Texas" ("Deep in My Solar Plexus"). (I often ran into Janis on the street, where we both hunted for cock every day. She usually advised me to get a better wardrobe and asked if I had considered a sex change. She died later that same year.)

Our merry band dropped acid or mescaline or psilocybin and tripped off to the Nocturnal Dream Shows in North Beach, where the Cockettes performed at the Palace Theatre on Fridays. Or dropped into the Stud to shanghai boys to audition as porn models. The ménage on Broderick Street was becoming well-known as one of the less skeevy portals into the porn business. Whenever I found a prospective boyfriend, Carol or Ferd went to work persuading him to fuck an actress on camera. I believed I was in love with Ferd, and thought if I let him co-opt my lovers, he would love me back. They were feckless lovers, anyway. It was amazing how instantly they turned straight for a little cash. A grimy curtain of sparkles hangs over these memories, probably an aftereffect of so much LSD. We lived allergic to daylight, when San Francisco felt like a graveyard under a bell jar. It had the muffled, overlit, queasy erotic gloom of *Vertigo*, with something in the grain of the daylight air a constant reminder that the drowsy dreamtime we occupied was sleepwalking to a bad end. Looking back, it was its own bad end: a narcotic lull in the motion of actual living, full of artificial, arbitrary dramas.

Ferd was a born leader. More so than was strictly good for him. Charismatic, more overtly willful than anyone else in his orbit, besides Carol. His mind was opulent, quick as lightning, stuffed full with the vintage furniture of Western civilization. His political notions were vaguely terroristic. If Carol behaved like a deposed monarch, Ferd suggested a restive Trotsky, marking time in exile with literary and aesthetic distractions. We aped his sensibility, his inflections, copied the style of his convoluted, Jamesian sentences. He would have liked to have been born in symbolist Paris, clutching a calla lily and gargling absinthe. He said things like, "We can't shoot with Sandy today, she's been *remanded* to the custody of her parents."

Murkily, however, Carol piloted his decisions, and seemed to color his every thought. It was vaguely understood that they would marry each other and pursue a different life, in an indeterminate future—at least, I think it was. For Carol, everything happening then was an aberration, some detour she'd taken out of perversity. She often withdrew in neurasthenic silence to the top of the house on Broderick Street, at which times a convalescent pall descended on the rest of us. Whatever we happened to be doing, an image of Carol, in dark velvet dresses with crepe de Chine collars, pacing in solitary rumination, one scarlet fingernail holding her place in a volume of Mallarmé, was never far from anyone's mind.

They were a formidable couple. Fond of elaborate, cruel psychological games, like characters in Laclos. They attracted

paramours and hangers-on like regents of a medieval court,
or, to put it baldly, they operated with good-cop-bad-cop team-
work, of a type I later observed in certain "power couples" of
the 1980s art world, and elsewhere.

Ferd dallied with people, to use an apt, archaic word. He
inspired a maniacal allegiance in those drawn to him, as he
was uniquely quick-witted, inexhaustibly charming, and at
twenty-seven possessed a quirky, haunted beauty of Strind-
bergian intensity. His looks became less beautiful, but more
disturbingly intense in later years. I barely remember the few
times we had sex. A rushed, furtive blowjob, usually, in Brando
Batty's pickup, the toilets of bars in the Castro, or the porn
theater where *The Straight Banana* ran for several months—I
was never alone with him much longer than a few minutes.
There were always, always other people around, competing for
his attention.

Carol seduced people into complicity with her grievances
against him. In that way, she alienated him from them instead
of her. She capriciously elevated one or another member of the
tribe to the status of "special friend," or turned on friends and
banished them forever, as whimsy dictated. Our coven cast a
Baudelairean spell over its accumulating human wreckage. It
was notorious in circles it touched for internecine intrigues,
secret liaisons, and Byzantine exit strategies, which everyone
in it continually formulated. It was not quite the Mansons, but
more like a diluted version of the sinister Lyman family on Fort
Hill in Boston, home of *The Avatar* underground newspaper,
the Jim Kweskin Jug Band, and Maria Muldaur—now long-
forgotten, anarcho-mystical artifacts of the 1960s American
underground. It was lumbering toward an unpleasant finale
from the outset, but we were young, gifted, and pretty in 1969.
None of us gave a damn about where we were going and hadn't
a clue what to do when we got there.

Somewhere in the course of the magical mystery tour, when summer died and the bay breezes turned chilly, I migrated from Hamburger Mary's to the child's room in the house on Broderick. Moving my belongings was simple. I didn't have any. Once installed, I found the room so constricting that I became a piece of animated furniture in the other parts of the house, most of the time in awkward orbit around Ferd and Carol.

I don't recall the exact wording of the note. It was tacked to a corkboard, obscured by other tacked-up messages, in a basement corridor of the Otis art school, when Otis was in the Wilshire District near my former apartment in the Bryson. Sheree Rose and Bob Flanagan, who pushed endurance art to a place where it really hurt, had given a performance seminar, in the course of which Sheree had nailed Bob's penis to a block of wood. Someone in the audience had fainted. I had been to many Bob and Sheree events. At least one person fainted every time. We were leaving the building when I saw the note, scrawled on pumpkin-orange paper in quivery pencil strokes: "When I die, I want to come back with a smaller penis." This struck me as the funniest thing I'd ever read, for some reason. I couldn't stop laughing about it. I said, "You have to look at this." Sheree had already seen it. It had been up there for a week. The boy who'd written it had hanged himself right after tacking it up for the world to read.

"He had a huge cock. It was the only thing about him that anyone cared about. It made him completely miserable."

Many men, I think, would consider a huge cock an enviable cross to bear, but obviously that kid hadn't.

three

I purchased the notebook I'm writing in last November at a stationer's behind the Goldoni statue on Ponte alla Carraia in Florence. The cover reproduces an engraving of the Santa Maria del Fiore basilica. It's tinted a warm, creamy beige. In real life the flat colors and rigid geometry of the façade of Santa Maria del Fiore resemble the visibly bogus building coverings sometimes draped over real ones under renovation. Walking past it at night feels like the dream so many people report, of waking up standing before a large theater audience without knowing their lines or what play they're in. Buñuel had that dream all the time. A lot of my friends have had it. I've experienced it most of my life, not only in front of a theater audience, and never as a dream, either.

Brunelleschi designed the dome of Santa Maria del Fiore. Brunelleschi also reposes in the crypt in Santa Maria del Fiore, among its many treasures: a Uccello fresco, a stained glass window Donatello designed, and one of the biggest gold crucifixes I've ever seen, by I forget who. This is not what I planned to write in this notebook.

After breakfast I leave the house, walk to Coppelia or down to the sea wall behind the Hotel Nacional and jot lists of "things to remember better at another time." I watch container ships glide across the harbor, follow pelicans streaking high above the fibrillating waves. They dive kamikaze fashion into the water, plopping back up to the surface like rubber ducks, beaks full of fish. The Malecón stirs up longing for things already lost to time, along with a thought that there aren't many things left to lose.

So far I've filled one notebook with my surprisingly legible, right-slanted cursive. It was often said to be identical to my mother's, though she was left-handed. Some of these new pages bear a sprinkling of names, followed by rows of associations. ("B., when S.C. came into the Mudd Club: 'She has that just-fucked look.'" "Story of the turd in the trattoria toilet bowl." "Karen F.'s pianist telling story about Nico.") Other pages reflect little broken-off efforts at narrative. The past is chaotic and slippery. I haven't had the Proust tea-and-cookie epiphany, or the flood of buried memories supposedly resurrected by odors. Havana is an encyclopedia of foul smells, it ought to trigger an avalanche of amazing flashbacks. But nothing doing. Or nothing much.

★

The house on Broderick Street was mined with unwelcome encounters: with Charles, who never budged from his wing chair and cast a disapproving eye on any scene that passed before him, though it was impossible to tell how much he grasped or paid attention to; with Steve, who began arranging candlelit feasts each week or so in an otherwise unused dining room, at which nebulous others living in the house appeared.

These included a stout black lesbian residing in a basement bedroom next to Steve's, an apparition in thick round glasses who resembled an enormous frog, and was somehow the local parent of an eerily silent, wraith-like white female child of eight or nine. An actressy, broad-faced blonde whose saturnine expressions hinted at lethal secrets concerning the future of each person in the house lived on the second floor, evidently sharing custody of the little girl, who was unrelated to either woman by blood. Carol and Ferd believed the child had been kidnapped in the middle past, possibly brainwashed into believing her parents were dead or had abandoned her to their care. After living on Broderick Street for a while I came to believe something of the sort too. The girl never left her guardians' rooms unaccompanied. We suspected she was drugged and kept in a stupor.

These women, bonded in witchy sisterhood, alluded in passing to New Age consciousness, hobbits, grokking, and black magic. They ascribed anyone's characteristics to an astrology sign, any event to some planetary alignment. Such occult blather was usually weak-minded drug talk, but something genuinely malefic lurked behind their mystic twaddle, sinister Cheshire grins, and breaching overfriendliness. We stayed aloof from them, gingerly deflecting proposals that we all "take a trip" together.

At Steve's impromptu dinners everyone claimed to have plans. Whether we actually spoke of them or not, we strove to convey, in some manner, that whatever we were doing at the moment was a well-considered step toward something more legibly responsible that we intended to do later. This focused ambition could have been an intention to cast a spell on Sleeping Beauty, or to corner the market in gold doubloons and pieces of eight. It didn't matter how unreal or implausible our plans were. Striking a goal-oriented note seemed imperative to everyone sipping Steve's Merlot and eating Steve's casseroles.

We were bent on reassuring Charles of our solvency, lest he conclude he had a houseful of deadbeat hippies on his hands. I don't recall the precise atmosphere on Broderick Street the week the October rent fell due, but paying it had become a pressing concern for Carol and Ferd. We three had dropped mescaline and smoked weed nonstop for a week without sleeping. People came and went through the house at all hours, as the crisp autumn days became shorter. Nights became interminable voids, the nightmare parties of North Beach and other dark attractions having diminished to precious few and far between. Desolating fog swept the chilly evening streets. In the starry night skies the cosmos seemed to wake from a long summer stasis and lumber into catastrophic motion.

Late one night the suggestion arose, almost certainly from Carol, that the rent issue might be quickly resolved if Steve, who had gone to the opera hours earlier with his ancient mother (then in seasonal residence at the Fairmont Hotel), were to discover my young, comely, prone, clearly willing naked person in his bed when he returned. Carol had a gift for suggesting things without feeling responsible for them after they happened. She could have given Mesmer a run for his money.

There began a not-terribly-contentious debate about it. Ferd weakly objected on grounds that I might well do it to please them, but couldn't possibly wish to throw myself under an elderly pederast, since I was nineteen, obviously naive, and clueless, however jaded I tried to act, and that *I had never even been fucked before*. He was, to my astonishment, moved to protect me, if not very forcefully—less from Steve, I sensed, than from Carol. He felt vaguely responsible for me. This made me uncomfortable, and somehow guilty. It was no revelation that Carol didn't care what happened to anyone besides Carol, an attitude I perversely chose to align myself with.

I cut into the argument and said it was no big deal, nothing to worry about, I liked Steve fine, I was open to whatever happened. It would be an amusing way to surprise him—I wouldn't testify in court about the hours leading up to my deflowering, but this was the gist. Perhaps I went through with it to defy Ferd's feeble concern, or to win points with Carol by proving I could be as cold and libertine as she was. I wanted to matter more to them than I did. If letting them pimp me out to pay the rent accomplished that, I was for it.

It was settled. The scenario felt lifted from a French bedroom farce. I crept down the basement steps to Steve's room, undressed, got in his bed, pulled the sheets up, and waited. Excited anticipation became drowsiness as hours went by; I nodded off.

I was wakened by a rapturous, throaty groan, and the simultaneous thrust of a sixty-two-year-old, unlubricated member deep into my rectum. I was pinned to the mattress by a gigantic, dessicated brisket. It didn't exactly hurt. It wasn't any pleasure, either. I didn't even understand what he was doing to me until he finished doing it. I'd read about it, and heard people talk about it, but it felt so unlike what I'd expected that I thought he'd substituted some innocuous household object for his penis. But no, apparently it was him.

The epilogue was strangely confused. I only viewed it from an oblique, distant quadrant of the first floor. The next morning Steve pressed a thick wad of cash into Carol's elegant grasp. Later, he came into the hall through the basement doorway, panting and dragging a large suitcase. He pulled it along the runner carpet and threw open the front door. A taxi idled in the street below. He announced that he was leaving for the Fairmont Hotel. "It's high time I went and killed Mother," he said as he left, his voice shaky. It was the last we saw of him.

Unstately, plump Arthur Ginsberg, gnomish magus of a media venture called Video Free America, materialized one evening, wishing to meet frowzy, bespectacled Lowell Pickett, grubby producer of *The Straight Banana* and other instant classics of modern porn. Instead he encountered us, vainly staking out Lowell's front door from his living room. We planned to shake down the elusive impresario for money he owed us. If that failed, we all agreed, we'd ask the dykes on Broderick Street to turn him into a toad, the way Kenneth Anger had done to Bobby Beausoleil for stealing footage from *Lucifer Rising*.

Arthur Ginsberg owned a prototype of the first portable video camera (the Portapak, which actually weighed a ton), which Sony was test-marketing and giving free to certain artists like Nam June Paik and Andy Warhol—and, evidently, to Arthur Ginsberg, whose resume consisted more or less

entirely of an "audiovisual poem" based on Allen (no kin) Ginsberg's "Kaddish." He was now searching for a real-life drama to document in real time on video.

In that prehistoric age of three-quarter- and half-inch magnetic videotape and analogue technology, it had not yet occurred to everyone on earth that his or her existence deserved recording more extensively than with silent home movies, snapshot albums, letters, boxes of memorabilia. A cumbersome first step toward "home video," the Portapak was too costly for most consumers. Its image quality was atrocious, not so much black and white as a spectrum of milky greenish gray that broke up into streaks and splotches of camera burn when the lens passed across a light source. Yet somehow the novelty of making something that looked like bad television inflamed the imaginations of a few people at the time, including us.

It's probably clear that we considered ourselves artists, although aside for Carol's one-hit fluke as a lyricist and

Ferd's first, arty porn movie, none of us had produced a thing to support this delusion. Here, suddenly, a chance to pretend that exposing the raw sewage of our lives, in a visually crapulous medium, was the same thing as making art! Obviously ahead of the times, by at least several minutes. We screened *Billy Rainey's Brother* on Lowell's projector, regaled Arthur Ginsberg with our unorthodox domestic arrangements and drug habits, and urged him to document us—sensing, I'm sure, that someone whose only previous idea had been to make a film of "Kaddish" was highly suggestible and clueless. This proved to be accurate.

However, Arthur Ginsberg was nowhere as suggestible and clueless as we were. A few days later, Video Free America commenced taping our days and nights on Broderick, our revels on the town (which had become dimmer and, frankly, listless since the summer). At once, the torpid formlessness of our lives took on a strangely bloated shape imposed by the incessant round-the-clock presence of bulky technical equipment and three large, overfed videographers pretending to be invisible. This was at least a year before the hit PBS series *An American Family* emerged from the haute bourgeois altitude of Santa Barbara.

Within a few days, I suspected, correctly, that Arthur & Co. planned on serving me up as a weird speck of lint on the central drama of Carol and Ferd. After a few days of taping, I made myself scarce. I wasn't in a happy place. This daily taping ratcheted festering tensions between Carol and Ferd and everyone associated with them into the desperate-looking exhibitionism of bad theater. People acted out to make the video more dramatic, more confrontative, more excitingly sordid. They exaggerated their squabbles into screaming matches, aired their ugliest thoughts about each other, told the camera things they should've confided to a psychiatrist, or a priest, or a diary with a deadbolt lock.

The Adventures of Carol and Ferd, as the finished masterpiece was titled, culled from thousands of videotaped hours, climaxed, like oatmeal heated to a boil, with the wedding of Carol and Ferd, which took place, without much notice, in the moldy Victorian parlor of the house on Broderick Street.

It was a travesty wedding, a macabre masquerade party, like the more perfunctory nuptials, a few years later, of Ingrid Thulin and Dirk Bogarde in Visconti's movie *The Damned*, officiated in this instance by a minister from The Process, a satanic cult noted for its vivid fashion sense. I don't know if it was a legally binding ceremony, or only looked that way. It struck me at the time as an obtuse publicity stunt, but then most marriages and weddings had struck me that way, and frequently still do. It was happening on a camera, for a camera, to give all the frivolous dissipation recorded earlier some earthly weight and a retroactive illusion of narrative momentum. I had withdrawn into a severe depression, and was practically catatonic.

All of hip San Francisco turned out for this spectacle: the Cockettes, Les Nickelettes, the Hells Angels, the porn stars du jour, a contingent of zonked hippies and scag freaks, the more party-crazed zanies of the gay underground. I only saw it later, in the video. Freaks were still pouring into the house when one of the Hells Angels—fortunately, I suppose, one of the less porcine, who didn't have the build of a small truck—threw me over his shoulder like a Visigoth looting a conquered village. He carried me like a potato sack down to the basement, where, uneuphemistically, with a diabolically acute sense of timing, he yanked my jeans down to my ankles, pushed me onto

Steve's former bed, opened his own pants, and raped me for several hours while the escalating noise above us made it pointless to scream. My rapist held the blade of a thick bowie knife under my chin until, howling like a rabid wolf, he came in my ass the first time. He tucked the knife into one of his boots when I stopped struggling against the fat, putrid-smelling cock hammering into my guts. Jacked on meth, he pulled out after spurting, immediately pushing his still-dripping cock into my mouth, indifferent to vomit that quickly spread everywhere, soaking the bedcovers. When it got fully hard he jabbed it into my ass again. Blood started pooling with the vomit; I lost count after four or five new penetrations, frequently passing out as he went on raping with gleefully relentless hostility. Snorting, groaning, farting, not for any effect on me, but as if he were fucking the corpse of something he'd freshly killed, making noises he undoubtedly made doing anything. The only words he spat out during those hours were: "Take the rest of the dick in that fucking faggot asshole," and alternately, "If I feel your teeth on my fuckin' cock I'll cut your throat open and fuck the hole, so better suck good." By the time charm boy finished, I had been unconscious for at least an hour and stayed that way for two days.

Carol and Ferd disappeared a week later. Without telling anyone except Arthur Ginsberg, they'd planned for months to skip to Chicago, resume abandoned degree work, and find jobs in academia. I segued from depression to schizophrenia. In a fleeting lucid moment I called my parents, begging for airfare to fly home. During a layover in Chicago, hearing voices, I wandered through the airport, shoplifting scarves and talking to the voices. The police came; quickly realizing that I would constitute a problem requiring onerous paperwork and time-consuming placement in a mental health facility, they escorted me onto my Boston flight instead of arresting me. Soon after it landed, my parents collected me. Then I had a complete mental breakdown.

A man in my neighborhood used to wish me dead whenever he saw me in the street, as he walked two enormous, snarling, unfixed male dogs. "I'll be happy when you're dead," he would say, or "Anyone can see you're shrinking with age," or "You'll be dead soon," and he would say this with a big goofy grin on his deranged face, not only on the sidewalk but also in the corner deli, the local bookstore, if he saw me there, never loudly enough to be overheard but distinctly, implacably, with obvious sadistic pleasure, in the matter-of-fact way that someone might remark on the weather, and this man, who was tall and bald and unpleasant looking, with eyes twinkling with insanity behind his thick glasses, had written a novel once, a neighbor told me, and believed his brilliance had not been sufficiently recognized, and not only wished me dead but wished many others in the neighborhood dead in the course of his dog walks, perhaps everyone he saw. These maledictions went on for two years, and eventually had their intimidating effect. After a time, whenever I left my building, I feared having to confront this person's madness. Life is difficult enough without this kind of thing. In Regla, finally, I paid a Santeria priest twenty pesos to make this person stop bothering me. When I got back to New York, a woman who worked in the bookstore told me the man with the dogs had died, suddenly, a week before, from a cerebral hemorrhage. I don't really believe the Santeria priest had anything to do with it, but for a moment it was nice to think so. "I wonder what happened to the dogs," she said. "Maybe he took them to hell with him," I said. "But look here," I said. "I can't help thinking there is a lesson in this. He wished me dead. He told other people he wanted them to die. And then his brain exploded."

four

When Abdul left the other day, I sat on the terrace smoking and looking at the trees for a long time. On the grounds of the Institute of Something or Other across the street, the leafage of several ceiba trees meshes with the plumage of a laurel whose roots have pushed through the sidewalk on Los Presidentes. This foliage obscures a cluster of royal palms, clusias, and soursops that forms a massive shape-shifting topiary when it shirrs in the trade winds. A ginger tabby lives behind the institute's perimeter wall, in a shady sunken garden.

A condor slipped across the sky. I picked chicken bits from the pasta salad Neyda had cooked for lunch and walked over to Los Presidentes and fed them to the ginger cat, who had settled under a bench on the *paseo* for the afternoon. At night, when swarms of mohawked punks and skinny Rastafarians roam the *paseo*, I feed the cats along Calle 21 between here and the Hotel Nacional. While the ginger cat finished her meal, I thought about Ferd being dead.

That spring eleven years ago, we drank on the Prado and the colonnades around the Capitolio with shady characters Ferd collected wherever we went. I couldn't follow the conversations, but I suspected the altitude at his end was absurdly high, since his sudden compadres were creeps intent on getting drunk at his expense and hoping to rob him if the chance presented itself. Ferd believed they were thirsting for an earnest discussion of socialism. For a brilliant person, he could be amazingly clueless about other human beings.

We ended each night at the cafetería on 23, surrounded by boys offering *pinga grosso* for "a little present," normally twenty US dollars and a T-shirt, or a pair of sunglasses. A comical, rage-filled transvestite calling herself Madonna, who looked like Lupe Vélez in *Mexican Spitfire*, pined for Miami, a BMW, and marriage to an elderly billionaire. She appeared on the stroke of midnight, artfully disheveled, as if she had been ravaged in a taxi minutes earlier. For the price of a cerveza, Madonna would introduce an emphatically willing, heroically endowed "nice, good boy," certifying, along with his *pinga* magnificence, that he came from a decent family and wouldn't steal anything if we let him stay the night. She was always truthful; she'd had them all before.

The straight-up *pingueros* were few then, among boys who are now Abdul's age (and, except for Abdul, have disappeared, or, like Madonna, died). Yesteryear's *pingas* came attached to quite honest young men, in fact, who were more interested in sex with a foreigner than the "little present" they received afterward. They were students, or held real jobs, and did, by and large, come from decent families. They more or less believed in the Revolution, despite the siren call of South Beach. Sex was fugitive, fraught with the thrill of the forbidden, though nothing was more commonplace. Now, when even Fidel denounces "homophobia," and the whole country senses the inevitable demise of socialism, sex has become a cold, private enterprise for the sons and younger brothers of vanished sweethearts. They prefer Nike trainers to affection. Their cell phones have become more involving than sex of any kind. Still, unless they are firmly attached to a rich man from elsewhere, they are totally available at the same depressingly low prices.

The ease of things astonished Ferd. Inevitably, he began to moralize about it from the world-improving altitude he habitually assumed. He befriended an acting troupe that held itself aloof from the cafetería's erotic commerce at a perpetual gin rummy game on a fast-food patio around the corner, where orange plastic tables were set up under the stars. It's now a swankier joint with an inside dining room and swishy waiters, a striving, hopelessly inferior Havana restaurant that makes you feel sorry for it.

The actors quickly exploited Ferd's guilty responsibility for the world's inequities. Sighing tragically over existential problems they attributed to excessive integrity and thwarted artistic genius, they required groveling persuasion before allowing Ferd to pick up the check for the entire table, every night. He welcomed that. He had an innate need to feel responsible for everything.

They were a pricklish, un-Cubanly snobbish group: six bland, despondent white males and one Trotsky-bearded mulatto, dominated by two lipstick lesbians *avant la lettre* who were not a couple and infused their theaterless theater company with an air of what I can only describe as chaste, imperious self-pity. I now have to wonder if my discomfort around them was justified, or simply a contrary attitude I struck in the face of Ferd's overdone camaraderie. The rummy table stood flush with the lobby of the Riviera Cinema. We soon knew the people working at the Riviera, their friends, their friends' friends: that's how things roll in Havana.

The woman who managed the Riviera had a *jinetero* son who attached himself to Ferd like a limpet. Ferd was love-struck in a matter of minutes. The boy didn't have a *pinguero* face or build, only the same hollow look of corruption and a doggish persistence that screamed stupidity. He was furtive and scrawny. His teeth were bad. His feet stank. He scraped a livelihood from just anywhere. I couldn't stand him. Ferd towed him all over the island with us in a rented Lexus.

In Santiago, their love story became unbearable. I couldn't look at that boy without hatred. Santiago featured an epidemic of conjunctivitis. Yellow snot seemed to drool from every eyeball. As soon as we arrived I rented a separate *habitación*. It was the screened-off parlor of a ground-floor apartment in the center of town. The owner was a drowsy old Buddhist who said it didn't matter at all who I brought to the room, as long as they weren't police officers. I pursued my own idea of fun for a week, escorted all over the province by a gang of punk rock *jineteros* in a 1950 Dodge convertible. We went to beaches and forts and ate a lot of seafood and fried bananas. One morning the Lexus pulled up to the curb with Ferd's paramour behind the wheel.

"Are you insane?" I screamed at Ferd, who looked crumpled and scared in the passenger seat. "We rented this on my credit card."

"I have to let him drive," he said plaintively. "I can't see."

I'm embarrassed by the tangled feelings, most of them childish, exposed during that brilliant, hideous holiday. I believed, for example, that Ferd took up with this charmless barnacle to reproach my beauty-freak whorishness. To show how more mature and meaningful his relationships were in contrast to my slutty one-offs.

There were other tensions at work, unresolved issues

between us. I think I'm working too hard to feel penitent about all this. I'm in danger of losing the thread. Santiago. The rental car. That finished it. Ferd wanted to borrow money. We were leaving the Lexus with the Rex car rental branch in Santiago. He'd spent himself broke during the trip, and couldn't afford his plane ticket back to Havana. He said he needed to buy one for the *jinetero* as well. He confessed that he'd already called Ricardo and Barbara, who owned my apartment, and asked them to wire two hundred dollars to cover that. He had more money in Havana, he'd simply miscalculated. I said the *jinetero* could catch a ride on a potato truck for all I cared.

"He should feel right at home," I said. "He has the brain of a potato."

It was infuriatingly cavalier, I told him, to ask Ricardo and Barbara for money. They were my friends, not his. They didn't have any money to lend anybody. He at least could have shown some trust and told them where he'd hidden his own money in the apartment, and had them wire that. Furthermore, wiring money on the island, even within the country, was a complicated, ridiculously time-consuming process. It would ruin their weekend.

To be bald about it, I thought it appalling for Ferd to presume upon people I'd known for years, in a way I would never have myself, behind my back. I knew they would send him the cash because they felt they had to, since he'd come to Havana with me. I didn't think he deserved their help. Or mine, at that point. I flew back to Havana alone and left him to figure out how to get the potato across the island.

My lack of empathy scandalized me at times. I couldn't control it. Ferd and I had stored up too much mutual resentment over thirty years to ever feel completely safe with each other. Now that it's too late, I realize I should have swallowed my loathing of that boy, if he made Ferd happy. Because he was abject and out of his depth, the boy tried to be invisible around me. He deferred to me like a servant, lit my cigarettes, pulled the chair out for me to get seated at dinner. At a certain moment my hostility felt forced and tiresome, but I refused to show him any kindness. Even when he held my head while I puked in a sink, one night where we'd dossed down in Trinidad de Cuba, I still couldn't look at him. He never asked for anything. He may even have loved Ferd, whatever that means.

Abdul remembers that boy telling him that he crashed the rental car into a telephone kiosk in Santiago after I left. Ferd never mentioned it. The insurance must have covered it. A few weeks later we left the island. We had stanched the wound, as we habitually did, imagining that it would never bleed again. Ferd flew to Mexico ahead of me. We met up at the airport in Cancun and continued together to LA. I slept at his place in Mount Washington for a few days, then moved into Highland Gardens on Franklin Avenue, where I had been living a few months out of the year.

Ferd returned to Cuba later in 2001, further proof that 9/11 didn't stop anybody coming here. He and the *jinetero* picked up where they left off, or it went bad, he never told me anything about it. The boy's mother no longer manages the Riviera Cinema, Abdul says. The family moved back to Holguín years ago.

All right. I was jealous. I had to know I was more important to Ferd than the *jinetero*. It came down to that pathetic insecurity, something from prehistoric traumas that wreak more havoc in the present than they did when they were fresh.

Ferd knew his time would run out a lot earlier than the national mortality rate. I know he counted on more than what he finished up with, who doesn't? He carried the terrible weight of approaching death for so long, though, that a dark outline displaced the air around him. He wanted to have one last love affair, and I made him feel like a fool about it.

★

North La Jolla Avenue. Winter. Rain falls every day. The ground-floor apartment resembles a monastery cell and rain turns it dank and bleary as a police holding tank. Los Angeles needs water, but the winds blow it south and it misses the reservoirs. The steady drought warning seems over-iterated and heavy-handed. You're not supposed to run the tap while you wash dishes. The toilet rule is, "If it's brown, flush it down; if it's yellow, let it mellow."

I scissor human heads and limbs from magazine ads and paste them into pages of "The Drunken Boat" in biologically impossible configurations. I'm making a collage book for a boy I met who was eating a burrito in the parking lot at Tommy's. He kissed me the way people kiss when they're in love. That was a week ago. He may not remember me now. His number is scribbled on a napkin stuffed in my wallet. Does he know who Rimbaud is? Does it matter? I can't tell what men I sleep with have in their heads. I meet them late and see the last of them before the sun comes up. I've sliced up the Thomas Brothers map I use to navigate the city, and arranged the pieces in a maze no traveler could follow.

A bookshop in the beveled corner of my building sells fetish gear and porn magazines, stroke novels, poppers, dildos King Kong would feel threatened by. If I look out the kitchen window, day or night, I see somebody in a parked car jerking off with a centerfold spread against his steering wheel.

Once a week I carry pillowcases stuffed with socks, underpants, jeans, and T-shirts to a coin-op laundromat beside a Winchell's Donuts in a strip mall. I skim the *Hollywood Reporter* and try to finish reading *The Rise and Fall of the Third Reich* as my clothes wash and dry. I smoke weed in my rotary-engine Mazda as it's towed through the car wash at Sunset and La Cienega. Afterwards my brain feels as scrubbed and clean as the windshield. I buy pre-ripped T-shirts at Tokyo Rose to wear to clubs. I drive to Watts, drive home, refresh my skin with an Aztec Secret Healing Clay facial mask. I reread *The Day of the Locust* in two hours, primp a little, then drive to the Detour in East Hollywood or walk to the Rusty Nail on Santa Monica Boulevard. I get drunk three or four nights a week.

I pick up a new person every night. This procedure is fraught with insecurity about my attractiveness. My willowy, fey look passed out of fashion a while ago, when the androgynous template slowly butched up during the disco era, becoming the present macho clone craze. I'm put off by the leatherman thing, handkerchief signals, big hairy chests and mustaches. If the Tom of Finland types aren't stupid as boiled okra, they give that impression in conversation. But there are usually some available persons in my acceptable range of maleness. Then it's down to whether or not they see me in a similar light.

When I can't think of anything else, I drive up Malibu Canyon, to a spot where the land disappears and the Pacific Ocean fills the entire view. The way sunlight shatters across the limitless water calms me with a sensation of infinite possibilities. This epiphany curdles into dread as I drive back down to Pacific Coast Highway.

At this moment I am twenty-five, and waiting for my life to start. The will to make this happen feels beyond me. I'm told I think too much, and have too many emotions. For some reason this terrifies people. In my own estimation, I'm emotionally blocked, stupid in practical matters, and cursed with an isolating intelligence that's worthless, "emotional" only insofar as I'm prone to panic attacks when my coping skills fail. I've gone into hospital twice for depression, which taught me where the safe line of sanity is. There is a threshold of self-neglect I can't cross without getting locked up. I have to carefully gauge how much unhappiness I can manage, as I seem to be a glutton for it, and still function. I've been on various psychiatric drugs for years. Lately I've dispensed with them, in favor of "self-medication."

I have no reliable idea who I am: I can be whatever somebody wants temporarily, if I glean a clear intuition of what it might be. I'm so solitary that roles I try playing for other people seem contrived and arbitrary. I'm uncertain enough of my existence to absorb nearby tastes and opinions, as if claiming them as my own will bring me into clearer focus.

I have a pinching wish for attachment. I don't know if it's real. It might be the product of movies and songs on the Top 40. Love is all you need, if loving you is wrong I don't want to be right, can't live if living is without you, this is dedicated to the one I love. In the bar ghetto I'm defensively cynical, or pretend to be. I don't fit with anyone I meet, except in a lubricious, sweaty, transient junction of organs and holes, a fusion of raw desires that discharge themselves with two spurts of jism. The guys I pick up

are impervious to emotional complications, intent on
probing a fresh body, pushing beyond conventional sex,
lab animals staging their own experiments. I do anything
I'm asked that won't kill me. I'm averse to grunting leather
ladies, but I'll go to a lot of the same places they do, taking
the same risks. I prefer a Ray Davies– or Bowie-looking
type to fist me, whip me, whatever, over getting mauled by
a human tank. It's not my usual thing. What I look for is
an abridged version of what I want: a no-fault fuck in the
parking lot of time between last call and the morning reality
principle, and a modicum of cordiality.

I live in a goulash of stalled creative yearnings, surges
of paranoia, fits of depression, frequent spells of drugged
euphoria. "I" is a blur, something like photo paper in a
developing tray. I swallow speed each morning in place of
a vitamin pill. I hear voices. I talk into a tape recorder
driving to work, preserving logorrheic routines in my head.
I'm inhabited by a cast of characters sucked from outer
space by amphetamines: a morbidly obese cab driver fond
of guava jelly doughnuts who gets his own talk show after
running over Al Pacino. Gary X, a gay-liberation terrorist
recruiting for a Baader-Meinhof branch in California. A
jilted studio hairdresser, May Fade, improvises verbal
suicide notes, digressing often to recall her work on
tragically hirsute or alopecia-stricken movie stars.

These cassettes circulate among some friends who send
mail art to Ray Johnson. This group calls itself Science
Holiday. Its members build exploding sculptures from old
chemistry sets. They occupy hard-to-locate pockets of the
city and depend on public transportation, the alternate
universe of the non-wheeled. Their main activity is cult
worship of Darby Crash and Devo. They have private
understandings that exclude me. I'm over-talkative and

GARY INDIANA   83

uncool. They tolerate my company because I own a car. It's depressing to be tolerated, but in this city even bad friends are hard to come by.

When the Baby June impulse strikes, I hit the piano bar circuit. Frequently I experience a compulsion to be seen and heard by total strangers. I would be in the right town for this actorish craving, if I weren't such an obvious fag. LA hosts numerous smoky lounges where anyone can grab the microphone and request a tune from a Vladek Sheybal look-alike parked at a keyboard. (In years to come, this safety valve for wage slaves degenerates into karaoke.) After many drinks, I have a pretty decent singing voice.

In all-black bars in Crenshaw, the piano players know Edith Wilson's "Mistreatin' Blues," and "I'd Rather Go Blind" by Etta James. At the Other Side, a wrinkle room in Silver Lake where the décor evokes a perpetually hungover, geriatric White Christmas, it's Lerner and Loewe, "The Night They Invented Champagne," or Cole Porter, "You're the Top"—an iffy choice given the clientele.

> You're the purple heat
> Of a bridal suite in use.
> You're de Milo's Venus,
> You're King Kong's penis.
> You're self-abuse.

My finale is an Ethel Mermanesque "There's No Business like Show Business," belted out with demonic abandon.

Is this anything I want to remember better? Yes. No. You tell me and we'll both know. Like everything irreversible and embarrassing, I'd like to remember it differently.

An unhappy-looking man in Ban Jelačić Square in Zagreb, tall, thin, with a thin black beard like a heavy pencil line along his jaw, wearing an "I ♥ Paris" T-shirt.

five

A red and black cargo ship crossing the bay this morning revealed a trick of perspective produced by the view from the back terrace. The rear terrace is cramped and perfunctory compared to the large, high-ceilinged one overlooking Calle 21. Its white wrought-iron chairs and matching table are smaller and stubbier than the furniture in front, crowded near the door of a storage room away from a squidgy alcove where Neyda machine-washes laundry and pins it up to dry, where there's another closet, full of sad children's toys, that Theodore Dreiser could describe a lot better than I can.

The back terrace has a jaw-dropping view, though, that would cost many millions to equal in Dubai or Hong Kong. It's a brilliantly swank spot to drink late-night cocktails and stargaze. At least one person campaigned to be my permanent consort after seeing that view. Many people who visit assume I own this place, even after I tell them otherwise.

The horizon behind the Malecón is fractured by faraway oceanfront high-rises. The ship's enormity, as it crossed the water and parts of it appeared in spaces between buildings, suddenly foreshortened the distance between this house and the sea. The ship's deck ran level with the tenth floor of the Girón housing project. This confusing revision of scale shrank the gray-blue expanse of water to the width of a narrow canal. The optical effect revealed my misperception of the earth's curvature, which I'd imagined more pronounced than it actually is, as well as a flawed estimation of my optical depth of field. I had wrongly imagined the view encompassed at least a third of the distance between Cuba and the Florida Keys. In reality, something less than a nautical mile is visible from where I stood. Abrupt and uncanny, the foreshortening caused a jarring feeling of exposure. I sensed the city visible from my flat looking at me at the same moment I looked at it.

The ginger cat from the institute hasn't appeared in three days. Last night, two police, one male, one female, asked to see my documents. Actually it wasn't a request. They found the leftover chicken I was tearing apart suspicious. They studied my passport as if they had seized a deceptive explosive in the nick of time, for the glory of socialism and the mother country. When I explained I was searching for my cat, though, they gave the passport back and began looking for her too. It was after midnight. Only teenagers on the *paseo* were about, strolling up and down in little cliques, passing rum bottles. One held his guitar the way you'd hold a toilet plunger, swinging it an inch above the pavement.

The sun is strong today. Chains of shredded clouds drift west on the trade wind. In a while, I will visit old acquaintances in the Colón Necropolis. Gaston Alvaro, Juan J. Musset, and four other firefighters killed in a blaze. Blanco Herrera-Ortiz, in a much-photographed marble catafalque. Familia Tamayo. Familia Borges. Ramón Cruselle Faura (1820). Francisco Gonzales y Osma (1882). The Revolutionary hero Cienfuegos, whose plane went down suspiciously a mile offshore. Calixto de Loira, the necropolis architect, who died in the great cholera epidemic right after he finished the place, becoming the first person buried in it. There used to be a densely freckled, red-haired caretaker, but no one there remembers him.

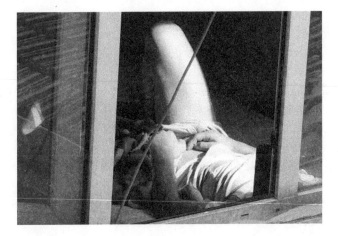

I promised to return before two o'clock. I think so, anyway.

Yesterday, sitting in the sidewalk café of the Hotel Telegrafico across from Central Park, I glimpsed a beautiful young man walking in the direction of the Capitolio. He glanced at me and slowed his pace, continued a few steps, looked back, looked away, walked a little further, then slipped into the French café, the name of which I forget, between the café of the Telegrafico and the terrace of the Hotel Inglaterra. His second glance was a familiar, unambiguous message of availability.

After he disappeared behind the plants bordering the French café, I wondered if he'd gone in there as a way of staying close to me without setting foot on the Telegrafico terrace, where he would not be welcome. I hadn't signaled any interest and decided he had probably been going to the French café anyway. A circumspect uneasiness that I had felt throughout the day returned in the form of uncertainty about whether this person was lying in wait for me, or simply buying a pastry. Often someone who solicits you turns out to be a can of worms. I decided to forget about him.

One type of person here, easily spotted in a crowd, is a young man or woman from the provinces who just got off the bus from Las Tunas or Ciego de Ávila and plans to find employment in construction or the service industries after a season or two as a sex worker. He or she might have family or friends in Havana but usually doesn't know a soul, and when the bus drops him or her off beside Parque Central, a new job is waiting a few yards away.

I thought the young man who went into the French café might be such a person. Such persons have an unspoiled aura that activates a futile and usually superfluous protective instinct. Havana is the least dangerous of cities. The only danger such a person faces is a cop demanding to see his ID card. A young man from the provinces, unless he wears a bespoke suit or other sartorial evidence of respectability, is often asked for his identity card. If it doesn't identify him as a native of Havana province, and he can't produce documents that explain his presence in the capital, they arrest him or drive him to the train station and forcibly send him back where he came from.

This medieval procedure was not in my thoughts as the young man in the French café began making faces at me. I mention it as a feature of Cuban society that promotes an atmosphere of dread and intimidation. This oppressive atmosphere varies in intensity at different hours of the day and in different parts of the city. Police comb through tourist districts with special care to expunge precisely the dazed, lonely, indolent-looking new arrivals from the provinces, to prevent them from "molesting" visitors.

However, this youth was safer in the café, spending money, than he would have been in the park, where I have often watched the police shake down young men who should have been entered in a beauty pageant instead of arrested. I didn't acknowledge him at first, but it seemed cruel to ignore him. He was making unusual efforts to get me interested. There was something puppyish and sweet about his face. From a distance he looked unusually guileless, a simple soul, even . . . well, quite possibly a bit retarded.

I stirred the coffee in front of me for no reason, lit a cigarette, opened the book I was carrying—Fontane's *Effi Briest*—and read a paragraph, found it impossible to follow, closed the book, smushed the cigarette out, looked at the yellow-domed pedicabs parked at the curb, flattened my hand on the table, rubbed my eyes, all the while processing a blizzard of aleatory thoughts, or half-thoughts, some having to do with aging, incapacitation, death, the possibility that cancer was slowly spreading through my organs. Another trail of micro-thoughts led to my parents, both dead, guilt, awkward episodes of childhood, my failure to ever convey my whereabouts to what remained of my family. Mixed in with this, a vexing suspicion about the state of my lungs, followed by a reel of mental images, featuring sodomy in all its miseries and splendors, a partial replay of my recent week-long search for a pencil sharpener in every conceivable and inconceivable place in Havana, snippets from a scene in Fassbinder's *Fear of Fear* in which Margit Carstensen washes down a handful of valium with a tumbler of whiskey . . .

I stared at the murky, greenish Adolph von Menzel painting on the cover of *Effi Briest*. I looked up. The young man's head and shoulders loomed over what appeared to be a bouquet of drastically pruned sago palms in the middle

distance. He grinned goofily, the grin turning his face into
a parody of a face. Then he vanished behind the plants. I
opened *Effi Briest*. I read. When I glanced again at the
midget palms or whatever they were, the young man—a
boy really, I now realized—sprang up at the same moment,
still grinning his face off, then dropped out of sight again.
He had evidently settled at a table in the French café. Soon
he began springing up to stare at me at one- or two-minute
intervals, like a six-year-old playing peekaboo.

I noticed that his flesh was a few shades darker than a
walnut, his hair black and short, like a skullcap. His features
were . . . smooth? Finely proportioned? It's easier to say
what he didn't look like. He didn't look at all like a hustler.
He wasn't delicate. He wasn't tough-looking. He didn't look
corrupt, or skanky, or furtive. The volumes of his face were
unemphatic, but pleasantly inflected, his head more oval
than square. His brown eyes were arrestingly deep. His
ears were smaller than they should have been. Unconsciously,
I had begun returning his looks with a series of increasingly
unnatural expressions reflecting my ambivalence about
looking at him. What if he was insane? All right. After a
half hour or so I gave in. I walked around the apron of the
Telegrafico terrace into the French café.

He sat at a little round marble table. He was not alone.
A strikingly skinny girl, whose stringy, brownish hair was
cinched at her neck with a red rubber band, sat across from
him gesturing with her hands, laughing, or more exactly,
bobbing her chin and opening her mouth as if she were
laughing uproariously, without making any sound. She wore
a tight, red faux-leather jacket, a patterned mid-length
skirt, zippered brown boots that reached to her crossed,
bony knees. A desultory face, an urchin prettiness, avid,
exophthalmic eyes. As I sat down, her lips pursed and

puckered in a series of knowing little smiles, her eyes moving
back and forth between me and her companion, who looked
sheepish, shy, but shrewdly involved in the moment.

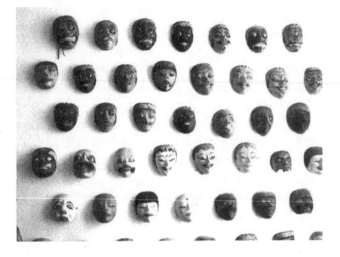

The girl was drinking soda from a can. The youth—I
don't know what else to call him, he wasn't exactly a boy,
not quite a man as a man is usually thought of here, i.e.,
married to a woman raising their kids while he shacks up
with a girlfriend—held an empty coffee cup in a loose fist.
They looked at me intently. For an unnaturally long time
we sat there, the girl smoking cigarettes, the boy, looking
feline, slouched in his chair, no one talking, as people went
in and out of the café and other people trod along the
sidewalk. Eventually the girl pointed at the youth, moved
the same finger horizontally before her lips, motioned at
her ear, moved the finger back and forth in front of her. I
understood: the boy couldn't talk or hear.

I pointed at her with a questioning look. With a series
of gestures that were not formal sign language, she indicated

some slight hearing in one ear, and her ability to speak, which she demonstrated by uttering sounds that were not exactly speech, but phonemic filaments whose longer vocables stuck in her throat as she tried to expel them.

After much awkward effort, we established that the boy wanted a date, which I already knew. His mutism excited me. It seemed to promise something besides the quotidian sexual exchanges so ubiquitous in this city. In minutes we were in a taxi, rolling down the Prado to the Malecón, across the Malecón to Avenida 23, up 23 to Paseo de Los Presidentes and down to the corner where my house is. We had sex after two Cuba Libres: rough, dirty, prolonged, intense.

His name is Mastiu, which I have trouble committing to memory, a fisherman working in Cotorro for the season. Next month his job will finish up and he'll go home to Santiago. He fishes from shore, at night, in high rubber boots. His boss sells the fish to restaurants. Mastiu has an insane ex-wife in an asylum, and a small daughter living with his mother, whose whereabouts aren't clear. It's not clear exactly where he lives, either. I picture him in Guanabacoa, for some reason, in a decrepit house with a Santeria room. He has difficulty spelling words as he prints them on a yellow pad we use when miming fails. He can barely write. I'm not sure he can read.

He has a cell phone, but I can't text him, since my US iPhone doesn't work here. I can't call him from the apartment phone, because he can't hear. Since the building door is sometimes locked, I agreed to look for him from the balcony after two o'clock. Since the gestures we used to communicate lacked a single unambiguous detail, I'm not sure he's actually coming at two, or coming at all. As he left yesterday he held up one finger and shook his head, then held up two and nodded emphatically. He soundlessly

whispered *"mañana"* many times before stepping onto
the elevator. But maybe he was saying "mama" or
"Managua." How could I be sure? I am going to the
Necropolis. On the chance that I understood him correctly,
I'm coming back at two o'clock. Or not coming back,
because a lot of things here that seem uncomplicated only
seem that way because I've overlooked some element that
makes them fundamentally impossible.

★

1976. The Bicentennial year, tall ships, fireworks. Death
toll from an earthquake in China, six hundred thousand.
Ulrike Meinhof hangs herself in her cell in Stammheim
Prison. Or someone helps her a little. Distant urgent events,
thrilling history you're embedded in like a questionable
semicolon, powerless to affect the annihilating progress of
the human species, only able to watch with a stricken feeling
of being deliberately left behind. Not only by the other,
cooler kids, but by history itself.
   Richard Hell and the Voidoids. The Ramones. Son of
Sam. Pol Pot, formerly Saloth Sar, becomes Genghis Khan
of Kampuchea. Mao Tse-tung, Howard Hughes, Max Ernst,
croak. These random subtractions from the swarm drag us
along in their wake and work us into funny shapes, or set us
on a dimly perceived trajectory. For instance: in Chatterton's
Bookshop, I instinctively snatch up the only copies of the
single editions ever published of *X Magazine* and *X Film
Magazine*. Both have materialized in Los Angeles along an
occult route. I discover in these one-off New York
underground papers, printed on cheap newsprint, writers
and artists whose intimate circles will include me in another
three years. My anxiety over the Red Army Faction trials in

Germany, the storming of the hijacked plane in Mogadishu, the sense that capitalism needs to be torn down and incinerated is mirrored on every page—nobody here discusses these things, or allows them any significance.

Some nights I sleep with Dane Eberstadt, an exterminator who lives in the Valley. I met him at Oki Dog. He was eating a burger and watching kids burn each other with cigarettes. He looks like a depraved surfer. His sun-bleached, messy hair has an acid-purple streak running through it and flops across one eyebrow. A lanky five foot ten, with something skewed in his face. His nose veers to one side where it was broken, a small deformity that makes him beautiful instead of merely good-looking.

Dane drives a pickup with big silver bifenthrin canisters mounted in back. His house off Lankershim Boulevard sags like a deathbed smile, the weedy jungle in front a busy airport for thousands of white moths. Blinking Christmas lights entangled in ceiling fishnets cast tiny pats of color over a living room time forgot, dabbing two incapacitated hippies sprawled on dumpster sofas. "This is Chester, that's Bob," the exterminator says, giving an unresponsive big toe hanging over a sofa arm a friendly pinch. A lean black kitty with white markings and one green eye, one blue, pads excitedly across the warped keyboard of an upright piano for Dane to stroke under her chin. He plunks out "Chopsticks" to see if either housemate is conscious. They could easily be dead. He doesn't encourage a lot of talk. He pulls me against himself with proprietary hands, kneading my ass with his fingers. His tongue feels like worn-down sandpaper in my mouth.

His bedroom is a vast Aladdin cave of candles, a waterbed that could cover a swimming pool. Reefer smoke and patchouli mask a cheesy smell of amyl nitrate. The bed's undulations continue long after we've fucked for several hours, a tactile pentimento of sex. I drift into dreams in which his penis is still inside me. We're in impossible public, places that could be airports or museums or some mongrel shape-shifting architecture where, in plain sight of other people, I'm attached to him like a screen door flapping in a thunderstorm. I wake up, or dream I've woken up, feel breath on my hair and a foot pressing into my leg. Under the beaded fringe of a faux Tiffany lamp a night table with a litter of lidless Vasoline jars, candle-wax splotches, a glass bong streaked inside with oily grime, an open, filigreed jewelry box full of crushable amyl nitrate lozenges.

The only books in his house are *Alice's Adventures in Wonderland* and *The Tibetan Book of the Dead*. Dane's history is Kentucky, Catholicism, two years of Army training. He used to be straight, or thought so. He's never played a bottom, though claims he wouldn't mind. He thinks he should take it up the ass sometime, at least once, "if I'm planning to be gay and all."

The size of his cock is startling. He jokes as if it's his evil twin, or the ventriloquist's dummy in *Dead of Night*: "Tell Stiffy where you want him to slap you." When he was in high school, "Kentucky girls impaled themselves on Mr. Stiffy." Later, Army friends took him to Nashville brothels, where they watched him screw hookers with his giant dong.

"I get off on people watching. No business like show business, right? But. I was not taking Mr. Stiffy on a USO tour of Vietnam." He arranged to get caught in flagrante homo at Fort Campbell, "with this butch bottom from Idaho. You can picture the disgrace. He wasn't even the type I'm attracted to. I'm more into the delicate, fem . . . *genre* like yourself. I'm not all man or anything, but I could still fuck a chick, if I had to."

"Why would you have to? Do you want to?"

"Sure. I mean, if she has a dick."

Dane is a footloose character. He calls me only when he wants sex. After a fuck he turns invisible for weeks, months. If I'm not home he rings another fuck buddy. He has them all over Los Angeles County. Guys he's met in bars, at swap meets, in Licorice Pizza. His sunny disposition is implacable. Years later, Ron Vawter, though a more brooding and reflective guy than Dane, is cut from the same cloth: former Army, former Catholic, nightstand poppers, crazy dick, easy come, easy go.

Dane's sleeping face is soft and untroubled, the face of someone well loved as a child, who still feels adored and protected by those around him. Unlike most people I hook up with, he's not neurotic, secretly hostile, or messed up on drugs. Or, if he is, I don't see him enough to know.

On weekends I sleep with him in the Valley, or else he sleeps at my place. He doesn't care for my apartment, which makes two of us. We fuck insanely, for hours at a time, rutting like dogs on steroids, all over our respective domiciles. We fuck the instant we wake up, fuck before and after foraging snacks from the refrigerator, fuck in the tub, fuck standing up in the shower, fuck slammed against walls, fuck to defy our own exhaustion, fuck until we're no longer sure if we're fucking or have fallen asleep and continued fucking in our dreams: a real fuckorama every weekend, enough that I feel internally damaged for days afterward. But we both have the miraculous recuperative powers of bodies under thirty. Occasionally we clean ourselves off and go to a movie or order Chinese food. It's nice.

I resent the wistfully possessive wishes that develop from this relationship. They're irrelevant, they bring sadness into it. They're sappy, romantic in a way that's lethal, drawn from bad fictions. There isn't any road map for homosexual relationships, and gay marriage hasn't remotely been thought of. But an obtuse desire for this strictly erotic liaison to evolve into a less parochial equation, something more social and public than sequestered in a bedroom, intrudes on what's otherwise an exhilarating mental enema and a country-simple good time. I have a million reasons to hate myself at this age. Yearning for clammy attachment tempts me to sabotage things, to suggest a different intimacy he doesn't want and won't put up with. One night I'm carelessly obvious about this wish, and he tells me exactly what to expect: "Ninety-nine percent of what I have to give you is going soft between my legs right now. If you need more from a boyfriend, you picked the wrong dude."

Dane accepts the world the way it is. I don't. Life is simple in his view. Any problem has a quick, visceral solution, or else it's not worth thinking about. I find it difficult to live. He's turned off by intellectualism and displays of strong feeling. We are wired differently. That doesn't necessarily preclude the intimacy I long for, but with him, it does. We treat each other fondly, often with great tenderness. But that's as far as it's ever going to go. My stupidity amazes me today.

"Why are you getting so agitated? You're a fucking Chihuahua. Relax. Slide down Mr. Stiffy, let him do all the work."

"I'm jumpy. It's my nature."

"You're jumpy because you take pills all day. You yip and babble in your sleep like a jumpy Chihuahua, on account of speed. I know you dream about dog food from a can. I hear you going *yip yip yip*. You know what you need? Quaaludes."

"I don't have a dealer for quaaludes."

"Sure you do."

He hops out of bed in his blond naked glory, rummages in a drawer, flings a baggie of round white pills at me.

"Take one now! Let it wash over you and carry you off to Neverland!" He assumes the voice of a detergent commercial: "You'll be glad you did."

"You think?"

"Take two! You'll sleep in a state of bliss!"

In my mind, for decades, hooking up the way Dane and I did was "profane" love, which followed no evolving narrative pattern, a thing in and for itself, like God or a black hole, existing outside normal time in an alternate continuum where personal identity dissolved in roiling puddles of flesh.

Anything that felt good could happen there, if the energy was right: Bob and Chester, Dane's housemates—essentially sweet, slow-witted, skinny guys with stringy beards and mustaches, cataleptically prone in the living room much of their semi-waking lives—did me occasionally at Dane's instigation, sometimes separately, usually in tandem, while Dane watched and shouted directions, a circus barker with an invisible megaphone ("Sit on his face—that's it, lick his asshole, but keep playing with yourself"), eventually joining us in a vaudeville finale. For a while, prowling the Valley and East Hollywood in his truck like a pair of serial killers, we picked up strangers at bars as they walked to their cars after closing time. On the huge, careening waterbed we plied guest lovers with weed and poppers to coax little fetishes and quirks from sealed-off rooms of their libidos. We assured them their secrets were safe with us, though later, when Dane and I were alone, we mimicked their peculiarities, aped the way they undressed, copied their segues between various acts, repositioning organs and holes, limbs and digits, repeating words and phrases they groaned or gasped out a moment before orgasm, exactly the way they had.

These escapades widened our repertoire inside the bubble where we knew each other more and more thoroughly as time passed. In other contexts we remained superficial acquaintances, two strangers at a restaurant or a movie theater stranded in each other's company by the unexpected absence of a mutual friend.

It wasn't what novels and movies and growing up with emotionally constipated parents had prepared me for, but nothing that happened to me ever was. The first sixteen years of life prepared me for absolutely nothing, actually. Long after I left Los Angeles, I still clung to a nebulous ideal of a lover who cared to know more about me than the fact that I had an unusually tight asshole and gave fantastic head. I fantasized about a domestic arrangement that would be a real story instead of a non sequitur.

In Los Angeles, I wasn't ready for the stoicism my experience recommended to me. I couldn't accept myself as a discrete being. I expected someone to mold me into something half me, half him. Later, it became clear that this blurred identity was only obtainable with people I never saw with their clothes on. In a related bolt from the blue, I realized that the only time I actually found melting together with anybody remotely pleasurable was when I had sex with them. I didn't want it as a daily, domestic state of things at all. I couldn't live with sexual lovers. I had, in fact, no real capacity for romance in that way. Only, now and then, with someone I cared about, felt tenderness for, could talk to, could sleep with at night if we first got sex permanently out of the way, and proceeded to have it exclusively with other people. By then I no longer viewed this as a terrible compromise with reality. It said nothing abject or horrible about me, either. Things were the way they were because, whether or not I acknowledged it, they were really how I wanted things to be.

Susan had tried hypnosis before, but we had both tried everything else, and she thought a group situation might work better than a one-on-one hypnotist had. We took a cab to an office building in midtown where roughly twenty people, mostly middle-aged, had assembled under fluorescent light in a room full of folding chairs. It looked like an AA meeting. The hypnotist vaguely resembled Lionel Stander. He explained the difference between the way hypnotists are portrayed in movies and how hypnosis "really works," leading the group through various breathing exercises and other physical adjustments meant to induce a receptive state.

"Now. When the thought of smoking enters your mind, replace that thought with another one: 'I need my body to live.' Because, you see, your mind can only hold one thought at a time."

Out on the sidewalk, we instantly scrambled for cigarettes and lit up. Puffing furiously, Susan said, "Are you thinking what I'm thinking?" "I think so. I'm thinking, 'I need my body to live.'" Susan nodded. "The minute he said you couldn't have two thoughts at the same time I knew he was full of shit."

six

~~Premature~~ *Impossible to write about Werner, who exerted such influence for 30 yrs, first through movies & later force of personality. Werner dead almost three years, missing person whose absence makes the world small and unbearable. "What now happens to my soul"—Magdalena's last words. Drawn to him by occult forces—plus Ila von Hasperg, Volker Spengler & Mostafa Djadjam—MD tried getting me to suck off Frederick S., the one whose hand got blown off in May '68, in my room at Luisiane that winter D.W.'s neediness made me so miserable.*

Need to meet Werner more urgent during stupid affair w Harald Vogel, worked for W on Weisse Reise. Maria Schneider. W a Byronic figure. I fell in love with his photograph. Thinner, prettier, more ethereal Oscar Wilde, cascades of silken hair framing long oval face. Not sure feelings were ever "sexual" despite sex. Felt complicity instead of desire. Harald's friend Robbie. Parasite coke whore. Came to Oblovitz loft near the Trade Center. Rosemary, Barbara, Oblov, Christophe. The week before John Lennon was shot. Dancing w Barbara to "Double Fantasy." Too much coke in the loft. Robbie supposedly producer of Harald's film, but H never made the film. Pinched, nervy face, bald as a boiled egg. Looked like a retired banker who repairs clocks as a hobby. Worst kind of German stereotype, thought it was a put-on but it wasn't.

I forgot all about him then 5 months later staying w

Valie Export in Vienna, phone rings, it's Robbie. "You said you wanted to go to Czechoslovakia." How did he get the number or know I was there. But I went. Shows up driving really battered white Mercedes. Vienna to Brno him the whole time full of Nazi opinions. Hated him suddenly & thought I should [something crossed out] & also afraid of communism. Wldn't let me go into Janáček Opera House. R took charge of everywhere we went ate everything. Karlovy Vary, Mariánské Lázné, Prague. Spas. Castles. Museums, opera houses, theaters, Soviet monuments. He hated to do anything and nothing interested him, was only interested in blabbing Hitlerite viewpoint of Slavic races & swimming in large municipal pool in Prague. Figured out he was not a film producer but a used-car salesman. Gave Harald $200 for Super 8 film that H. spent on drugs. Mercedes battery already faltering in Vienna & had to be jump-started every time he turned the engine off. ~~incessantly complaining, narrow-minded, grossly opinionated turd,~~ Psychotic and cheap, two bad qualities. Told stories about Hitler, where Hitler liked to drink beer in Munich, how Hitler was right about invading these unimportant countries because many Germans living in Poland & Czechoslovakia. Always insisted on cheaper hotel, cheaper café, cheaper restaurant than anywhere I wanted to go. Pieces of car fell off all over the countryside. In cities deliberately parked where getting battery charged by some total stranger he flagged down caused maximum havoc blocking traffic.

All R ever ate was sausages from street vendors. Thought seriously about murdering him w tire iron dumping his body in a lake & driving to Munich. Insisted we sleep in the car several nights to avoid paying for hotel. One time woke up & saw we were parked next to some top secret military installation.

We stopped speaking unless we had to. Suddenly he said we had to go right away to Munich which was all I was hoping for already for 10 days. Cristina the photographer (saw her 10 yrs later at Chateau Marmont where she was

*frosty to me) was not at her apt where I was supposed to
stay, went with R to his place praying to god I wdn't have
to sleep there, it was also surprisingly dirty & messy for a
Nazi apartment. He had no alcohol only ½ bottle of Cynar
that shit made from artichokes. I drank the whole thing
& then R says, "Well let's go to the beer keller," meaning
Hitler's favorite hangout, which he is still eager to show
me though we hate each other's guts at this point, but
führerkeller ist geschlossen so we go to Harry's. The Harry's
maître d' can see that R is a complete loser so gives us a
bad table, downstairs. We drink for four hours R the whole
time being a total asshole even singing "Horst Wessel Song"
in a low voice.*

*When we leave & go up that spiral staircase to the main
floor, I see Werner's hat at a table in the window, I know
it's him as he wears that hat in all his photos, I lurch across
the bar, fall over the table sending glasses plates knives and
forks and bottles flying, Werner jumps up rescuing his glass
from getting smashed. I land on my back and look up stupidly
from the floor: "My god, you're Werner Schroeter"—"I was
Werner Schroeter," he says—we somehow got rid of Robbie
& went to apt of that actress Annette—the one Magdalena
said, "If Annette were sitting here she would have drunk
that whole bottle already"—little terrace overlooking the
Olympic park, lots of wine. Werner took one shoe off &
rubbed his foot through a thin white sock. Couldn't tell if
we would sleep together or not.*

*That was when people who became important friends—
Daniel Schmid, Ingrid, Dieter, Jean-Jacques, Magdalena,
Veruschka—came into the picture, all in about 6 months,
all unique in the world. Werner generated euphoria if he
accepted you & for maybe 5 years we understood each other.
Later not so consistently though there was still love &
affection despite melancholia. No, I can't, not yet, if ever.*

*Robbie is probably 70 now & selling used Mercedes in
Bogenhausen. It wouldn't surprise me at all.*

No *New York Times*. No high-speed Internet. No *Desperate Housewives of Atlanta*, no *American Idol*, no *Dancing with the Stars*, no Kardashians, no Donald Trump, no Tea Party, no NRA, no Rite Aid, no Chase Bank, no Merrill Lynch, no Goldman Sachs.

Of course it's coming, coming here, coming soon, the gathering tsunami of Our Kind of Capitalism. iPad, iPod, YouTube, Buy It, Love It, Fuck It, Dump It, Buy a New One. The people who sell all this shit say it's what people want, and they're not wrong. But if people knew what they were in for, their heads would explode.

"What can stop it?" A Cuban painter asked me at a dinner a few nights ago, looking at a photomontage of Future Havana, plastered with giant advertising billboards and buildings wrapped in corporate logos. Yes, it's coming. Not yet, but soon.

"I haven't got any idea. An ecological catastrophe?"

"That is the ecological catastrophe."

The *pingueros* at Bim Bom whip out cell phones when there's a lull in the scramble for tricks. They can't usually afford to call Miami or Europe, so run their minutes out calling each other while en route to exactly the same place, texting and blabbing. When their minutes have run out, they watch porn loops on their phone screens. The current favorite is an astonishingly large black cock pumping the cunt of a glazed-looking white woman with runny mascara and pink lipstick. She looks completely stoned on heroin. The man growls, in thug-inflected English, "I'm gonna cum, I'm gonna cum, I'm gonna cum, I'm cummin' now!" He pulls out, splashes jizz on her tits, the scene restarts with no visible splice. The loop is a skanky metaphor for the standard life of a *pinguero*, minus the dull transitions, which is probably why they stare at it over and over, laughing sardonically, spellbound.

A man at dinner told me he lives on Formentera, but travels incessantly. He can't stand being in one place. We had that in common. Others at dinner were current New Yorkers originally from Montreal and Australia, and a couple from New York living here off a fortune from junk bonds. They had the hearty, confiding laughter of people engaged in an ongoing criminal enterprise. The New Yorkers from New York came here to take photographs. They have been east, to Trinidad de Cuba. Today they're driving west, to Pinar del Río. On safari, apparently.

D. disputed my idea that the convertible peso has restored a measure of national self-esteem after the blows of the Special Period and its long aftermath. I said it had to have been demoralizing, in the years of the dollar economy, to use a political enemy's coin of the realm. D. was impatient. If he sells a painting in Miami, he said, it's paid for in dollars, but before that turns into usable money here, thirty percent of it goes missing in tax and conversion charges. All right. National self-esteem is a pretty vapid concept at the best of times. Especially at the best of times, come to think of it. When I changed a lump sum for my rent, I lost seventy dollars in the process. I hoped it made somebody feel better. This scam to sock hard currency into the treasury, though, is probably even more shortsighted than the Argentine sleight of hand twenty years ago, that insisted one peso equaled one dollar. It might feel fractionally less slavish to be more desperate for CUCs than dollars, of course, but the real problem part is the desperation.

There was a lot of talk of DSL, the importance of getting it installed throughout the country as soon as possible. I understand that. But the technology is addictive, and humanly wasteful, I believe, out of all proportion to its benefits. It warps the way people think, destroys their attention spans. Corrupts many other, more important things like imagination and creativity. It's ruined Japan, China, the US, Europe, and Scandanavia. Probably Chile, Brazil, and Argentina, too. It will be tragic when it wrecks Cuba, turning these lovely unhappy people into screen-gazing, antlike, unlovely, happy robots.

The man from Formentera said Formentera is entirely WiFi'd. It could be that the beautiful places will still offer too many tangible physical pleasures for the masturbatory virtual ones of the Internet to replace them. But I remember what happened in Hydra the year that island got TV: all the houses suddenly sported aerials. At night, every living room window filled with a trance-inducing cathode glow. The villagers abandoned outdoor chess and quoit pitching in the dusty evening lanes. They gave up watching the sun dissolve behind the Peloponnese dusk from the harbor cafés. In spitting distance of the wine-dark sea, they stayed in their whitewashed stucco cubes, watching reruns of *Matlock*.

Of course no Greek peasant or Tuscan shepherd primarily views his domain as glorious and exalting. He's organically part of it, for him it's utilitarian, natural in a different way than what a poet or a tourist celebrates as transcendent and "natural." Still, it takes a lot of social engineering for him to ignore it altogether. After escaping the dinner, I went to the Malecón, where one of my *jinetero* friends, finishing a pint, tossed the bottle onto the rocks, sighed heavily and said, "Isn't it beautiful here, with the wind and the ocean?"

The man from Formentera said that while he can't do everything he'd like to do, he's okay with just never doing anything he doesn't want to. I think that's what many of

us half-lucky people finally settle for. It's hardly catastrophic. Most people spend their entire lives doing things they don't want to do. And when you take a gander at the world we live in, it looks it.

He said he hadn't planned to live as long as he has. I guessed him to be forty-seven or so. Like me, he has to improvise as he goes along. At my greater age it's a dicey way to continue, fraught with the chance of sudden impoverishment long before the body gives up the ghost, among other horrors. I expected to be dead by forty, then fifty, then sixty. I don't wish I were, but after a time, extinction doesn't hold the same terror that it does at twenty—only the hideous ways that it usually happens, unless you die in your sleep.

★

Punk rolled into Los Angeles after its peak wave had already broken in New York. At first, we consulted flyers at Licorice

Pizza or Chatterton's Bookshop to catch bands like the Germs and the Deadbeats at Whisky a Go Go or the Palladium, or saw them at loft parties or clubs that opened and closed in one night in derelict warehouses out beyond Union Station. After the Masque opened in a basement off Hollywood Boulevard, Zero Zero and other official punk dives sprang up. Club Lingerie, a venerable R&B spot, came back as a punk venue. Later, cash-strapped Chinese restaurants, Madame Wong's and Cathay de Grande, turned into music bars that happened to serve egg rolls and chow mein.

I vaguely knew Tomata du Plenty of the Screamers from his early Cockettes days in San Francisco, and sometimes partied with musicians from The Nerves and the Circle Jerks. The bands had a potent negative glamour that drew me into a tireless nomadic audience: people who showed up for anything because there was nothing else at all going on in Los Angeles. The audience was as much the show as the music, raw sound that drilled into the brain and was less important than what the players wore, what they did with their bodies on stage. Everyone competed for the most fucked-up reputation, the most suicidal carelessness with drugs, the most gratuitously hostile behavior. Yet punk musicians and followers I got to know personally were touchingly sweet, highly intelligent, and un-materialistic to a Utopian degree. Damaged in one way or another, but who isn't?

I clung to the sidelines, watching. I admired the club people. They weren't dumb. They knew time was roaring past. They'd never be young again and claimed the moment in a frontal, risky way. I couldn't identify with them entirely. I had a day job. I was noticeably gay. The official sensibility was anti-homo, though most people in the scene were sexually flexible. They kept the homosexual side of things veiled, or theatricalized it with a nasty mockery that left room to speculate that they were putting it on. But they were much less squeamish about throwing bottles and carving up their own skin than I was. They were often semi-closeted fags; I was a semi-closeted punk. As was later the case with the Mudd Club, if you remembered what you did at the Masque, you weren't there. I have sunspot memories of shooting meth with Dane, falling facedown in the inch-deep muck on the Masque floor, pogoing like a gear with missing teeth, getting clobbered watching a brawl, a flying singer landing on me in a mosh pit. Sometimes I went home alone, sometimes I jumped in the car with ten people, of various genders, and drove to listless orgies organized mostly for more drugs and booze. Parties started after sunrise, meandered on in spacey pointlessness until late evening. Then drifted back to the clubs and restarted the spin cycle. All memories of that period run together, as a long vacation in a country no longer indicated on any map. Recently I was startled to discover that that vanished world, even my slight presence in it, had been amply documented by various pack rats who'd preserved the ephemera, recorded the club dates, noted the names of the bands and fans—there are more histories of Los Angeles punk, I think, than accounts of the Mudd Club, CBGB, Tier 3, Peppermint Lounge, Interferon, Limelight, and the other clubs that came and went in New York during my first years there, in the late 1970s and early '80s.

In November, Exene Cervenka from the band X moved in down the hall on North La Jolla and turned the rear apartment into a 24/7 mosh pit. The really gruesome noise kicked up anywhere between three and five in the morning—ironic noise, somehow, since it came in a deafening blast of EPs that bands I scrambled to watch at the Masque or the Whisky had recorded.

I hated asking Exene to turn it down, not just because she never did, but because complaining about it placed me on the asshole's side of some line of defiance, marking me prematurely old and out of it. Los Angeles punks weren't particularly rude or hostile to people they didn't know, but Exene was, and I hated her.

Whenever Dane stayed overnight, sudden brain-rape by Exene's speaker system drove him nuts. "I'm going over there." "No, don't, she'll turn it up louder." "Then I'm calling the cops." "Then those people will spit on me every time they see me! It's easier to move out." "You should move anyway, this place is depressing." "All right. I'll start looking around." "I know a place downtown you could probably move to. The Bryson. It's like a hotel, so you wouldn't have to pay a deposit or wait till the end of the month."

I ran into Exene and her gang on the sidewalk the day I moved out.

"You're moving? What a drag! *We'll miss you!*" Strange to say, they sounded sincere.

On an airport immigration line in Istanbul, the couple ahead of me debated which passports to use. They each shuffled five, like cards in a poker hand, all issued by different countries. Their voices were postcoitally blowsy. They asked if I'd been in Taksim Square the night before. They had been sprayed, it turned out, by the same tear gas I'd walked into three blocks down the street. Like me, they'd spent all night rinsing their eyes, and now could have easily fallen asleep on their feet.

"We just got married," the woman confided, making a little snort, as if they shared a few doubts about whether it had been such a great idea. She was forty-ish, dubiously blond, pale, strong-chinned, green-eyed, pretty, of unguessable nationality, wearing a wrinkled Chanel suit and no makeup. Her partner was youthfully loose-limbed but paunchy, quite a lot older, possibly Lebanese, with soft gray eyes and a stippled, whitish fringe along the edges of his thick black hair. One striped aubergine shirttail fluttered at his zipper; the other was stuffed carelessly into his pants.

He was trying to be amusing and, unlike most people in airports, succeeding.

"Guess where we're going," the woman quizzed with mock haplessness.

"Cairo, jewel of the Nile," her new spouse chimed in, rolling jaded eyes skyward at the ironies of travel.

There had been rioting in Cairo for five days, since the military coup. I had a half-conscious flash that this couple wasn't blithely jet-setting at all, but testing a much-rehearsed script for incipient snags, a fiction close enough to reality to pass unregistered in public. The immigration officer waved them forward.

"And then, what the hell," the woman laughed as she walked away, "Beirut. How's that for a dream honeymoon?"

seven

Even here, where no common vectors of real-time information exist and the world outside thins to a trickle of dubious news in Granma ("Venezuela Expects to Be Agro-Superpower by 2015"), the existence of an outer reality creeps into the charmed daily stasis. Last night, at P.'s house, while she was busy with a tiki-torchlit philanthropic garden party, I was left alone with her precarious dial-up Internet connection, Coca-Cola, and a bottle of Havana Club. I had the unwished-for opportunity to see an article about me in an American magazine, circa a month ago, that burnished a widely cherished recent myth of the 1980s— not so much my myth, but the myth of a protean "downtown" Manhattan, held to have been a great churning centrifuge of creativity fueled by the Mudd Club, Studio 54, punk rock, performance art, et cetera, et cetera.

A sentimental myth, slightly true. A lot of people devoted time to other things besides fucking, drugging, and partying themselves blind in clubworld. New York was more interesting. It wasn't a giant suburb of nothing yet. I was young. Still young. Barely. By 1982, though, a hamster-wheel culture of recycling and imitation was well underway, in appropriated art, sampled music, postmodern architecture—the idea of originality had begun looking questionable.

Maybe the human race, the white part of it anyway, had run out of things to be original about. The Manhattan makeover into a sterile tourist resort was encroaching, one neighborhood at a time, building by building, block by block, assisted by the art world, which planted itself in various neighborhoods that quickly became unaffordable by ordinary people and unlivable for even well-off adults. I arrived at the tail end of an era when New York had remained basically unchanged for thirty years—a real city, a dangerous one for the unwary transient, feared and detested by the rest of America. The ersatz, provincial, "post 9/11" New York is a holiday camp for university students and a pied-à-terre for Chinese billionaires, a place any young painter, writer, or musician would be wise to avoid, since it's no longer possible to live there on slender means.

The writer of the article phoned me out of the blue several months ago, describing himself as "a big fan," intent, he said, on making a younger generation appreciative of my work. After several minutes on the phone, I gleaned that what he meant by "my work" was the art criticism I wrote for three years in the mid-1980s in the *Village Voice*. He hadn't read any of my subsequent novels, or collections of essays and reportage, most of which have lately gone out of print.

I smelled disaster, but gave him an interview anyway, on the condition that he read something substantial of mine beforehand, not a bunch of yellowing newspaper columns I never republished and haven't cared about for a second since writing them a quarter century ago. I'm sometimes imprudently swayed by Ross Bleckner's old mantra "ink is ink" when someone proposes to spill some about me, forgetting that ink can hurt all the same. Especially if you're dumb enough to talk to a journalist. I have been a journalist, so I know.

I'm beyond feeling hurt by other people's opinions, I think, but how deeply, seriously skewed some of this is. The writer inserted obscenities into my quoted answers, making me sound raving and bitter, or, worse, an old person trying to sound hip. Brilliant. He says I look older than I am. A matter of opinion, and so what? He includes some gratuitous insults from a Canadian filmmaker whose basic claim to fame is that he was the first person in Toronto to wear a nose ring. Someone I met exactly twice, twenty years ago, when I was in Toronto with William Burroughs. No word from anyone who knows me. Fine. My life in a few paragraphs that size me up and judge me.

It's not exactly *The Lost Honour of Katharina Blum*, but it isn't how I care to be depicted, either. The photographer cropped my picture exactly where he said he wouldn't. He moved the light when I wasn't looking, accenting my wrinkles. I still can't accept being old. "It happened too fast"—famous last words.

Apparently I mentioned times long ago in California. Reading this magazine's garbled version of whatever I actually said brings up more memories of Ferd, and others, but what can you do? Memory is partial, colored by mood and contingency. The key is to remember clearly, but it's not possible. Conversations dissolve into mist. Interiors turn spectral, people lose their definition. I took a photo of Ferd standing in the surf in Pinar del Río, but I can't find it. There are YouTube videos, Ferd receiving a citation from the mayor of Los Angeles, but by then he was wasted from liver cancer, and looked awful.

After they invented protease inhibitors, Ferd could wear pants that weren't beige for the first time in a decade. I wonder why, of all things he ever told me, I remember him telling me that? We come into the world shitting ourselves, we often leave the same way, but why dwell on it?

Strangely, the general tone of the article is admiring, despite its possibly uncalculated, patronizing tone. Admiration is widely imagined to be a positive feeling, but often turns out to be toxic. Besides the obvious matter of stalking, there is the question of approbation for the wrong reasons, and the subsequent disillusionment. There is the element of envy, and *All About Eve*, and the easily reversed loyalties of crackpots, and the lack of reciprocity involved in hero worship.

It wasn't only the article that sent my mind running along this route. Elsewhere in the room, P. had placed an artfully casual-looking pile of thick art books, among them Annie Leibovitz's *A Photographer's Life*. I had a testing, dirty sensation as I slid it out of the pile. I can truthfully say that little that interests Annie Leibovitz interests me, but I knew this book contained, among the celebrity portraits she shoots for *Vanity Fair*, many pictures of Susan Sontag, taken after my friendship with Susan ended. I knew the book featured pictures of Susan's dead body. They had been "controversial" when Leibovitz first showed them, though Susan had doubtless consented to have them shot. A kind of pornography, unfortunately a kind Susan and I shared a strong predilection for.

I was surprised to hear, when we were no longer friends, that Susan had befriended various new people like the dreadful, self-appointed widow of Fassbinder, Juliane Lorenz, and Marina Abramović, an artist the Susan I knew considered ridiculous—but then again, Juliane is powerful in her own ill-gotten realm, and Marina is now a huge Art Celebrity. Susan often cultivated people she privately held low opinions about, if they were famous enough. The larger surprise was Annie Leibovitz herself—on many long-ago occasions, a prime target of Susan's disdain for the crassness of celebrity culture. Susan loved to parse the difference between "fame" and "celebrity"—people were famous for doing something, she opined, whereas anyone could be a celebrity for any reason at all: celebrity was a transient thing, fame a lasting condition. This doesn't quite hold up. Today the famous are perhaps more quickly forgotten than celebrities, who, if they do nothing else, work tirelessly to stay in front of the camera flash.

I flipped directly to the death pictures. Susan was hard to recognize in the bruised, bloated carcass. So formidable in life, so insistent on her uniqueness. And here she was another slab of livid meat, like every other corpse.

I wasn't surprised by the ressentiment apparent in so many of Susan's obituaries. She was exasperating, often cruel, and, in a less than endearing way, oblivious to the impression she made on other people. She never stood away from herself to question her motives, or to consider anyone else's point of view, or their feelings. She thought other people were stupid—her friends were only tolerably less stupid than the general run of humanity—and never imagined they could be less than awestruck by her relentless display of intelligence and erudition, or that anyone could see behind the carapace she projected, from which every utterance was an imperious defense mechanism. She had an uncontrollable need to prevail in any argument, and bullied people she disagreed with, often out of personal animosities she wouldn't acknowledge.

I was regularly exhausted by her limitless capacity for admiring things. She was perpetually "moved" by this Japanese film director, "exalted" by that lesser-known Janáček opera, "besotted" by the contortions of some ballerina. When the pleasure of her company segued into pedantry, I usually glazed over. I could be pedantic, too, but . . . I once told her bluntly that this need to be exalted every minute of the day was terribly draining for people who had to pretend to be exalted along with her. Susan took, as was her wont, umbrage. It wasn't her fault if people were lazy and unadventurous, didn't care to eat a hundred-year-old egg or plod through a thousand-page Hungarian novel, though for the life of her she didn't understand why people were so lazy, though no doubt it had something to do with *television coarsening their sensibilities.*

It was impossible to like half the things Susan claimed to find marvelous. There was something freakish about the vastness of her enthusiasms and her habit of classifying them, grading them, scoring them, boxing them with calibrating adjectives. She feigned astonishment that you hadn't heard of something so arcane that absolutely no one except Susan had ever heard of it. Sometimes it was something really wonderful. More often, it was pointlessly demanding and trivial. On one hand, I was grateful for a friend whose appetite for reading was even larger than my own. On the other, I found her mentoring urge, expressed in the pushy demand that I absorb any arcane cultural phenomenon she happened to think of, an oppressive generosity.

She worked up to her exaltations with an eye to impress those around her with a depth of feeling that seemed a bit dramatized and artificial. It took formidable willfulness for her to cry at the end of Vigo's *L'Atalante*, I thought, when she had already seen it thirty times. No doubt she was moved all over again, but why? Because *L'Atalante* is a moving film. On the same syllogistic principle, X's poetry is great because X is a great poet, et cetera, et cetera. At

times, Susan resembled one of the face-pulling
schoolchildren in Gombrowicz's novel *Ferdydurke*,
incarnating lofty sentiments by striking noble poses. Like
the chalk-white, avuncular bust of Salvador Allende down
on the *paseo* on Los Presidentes, one arm raised heavenward
in a permanent access of revolutionary fervor.

Transports of ecstasy were a vital part of her image.
She disliked being called a critic, yet her eminence derived
from her unusual ability to bestow importance on other
people's books and movies, and on the perception that she
was more intimately familiar with the vast realm of culture,
and hence more discriminating, than anyone else. Susan
heaved from one enthusiasm to the next, a storm-tossed
vessel calling in at every Port of Epiphany. She wanted you
to see that she appreciated things more fervently, more
insightfully, more . . . well, more *movingly* than you did.

She flew to Europe once or twice a month, to see a
museum show, an opera, to hobnob with the cultural brand
names that decorated European journals of opinion and
literary quarterlies. I saw her in Paris, in Rome, went with
her to dinners full of film stars and theater people and the
cream of the intellectual crop, and all these people viewed
her as a sacred monster, an American anomaly who hoovered
information up and then did battle with it, battle with many
negative forces in the world, of course, but also, perplexingly,
battle with her friends, her colleagues, and most cruelly
her lovers, whom she regularly embarrassed and humiliated
by catching them out in an innocent stupidity, some
statement that exposed their limitations after Susan had
seized on it and held it up for ridicule.

In New York you could find her at the most out-of-the-
way screenings and performances, front row center, being
moved and exalted and besotted by everything from

Sophocles to Betty Boop. If she liked something, she watched it every night it appeared, forming in her mind those terse, laborious endorsements that served, for many people, as a certificate of top quality on a book jacket or a movie ad. An ideal evening might include a play at La Mama, dinner in Chinatown, followed by a film at the Bleecker Street Cinema, with a midnight kung fu double feature in Times Square as a nightcap.

This chronic aesthetic gourmandizing filled her with a histrionic rapture that required live witnesses, I suppose one could say, to the showy movements of her soul. More prosaically, she contrived to be admired for the powerful effect the higher things in life had on her.

She hated going anywhere alone, hated being trapped with herself. She even wanted people around when she was writing. This horror of solitude aside, the world felt more real to her when other people were in the room. When she discovered something, she wanted to share it right away. "That way I have my pleasure and the other person's pleasure, too," she said.

Susan often expropriated her friends' discoveries as hers, claiming, after the fact, to have come across something years before "getting to know it again" with someone who had actually introduced whatever it was to her. This peculiar habit of revising history—history, moreover, of no consequence to anything except an implacable vanity—made something as simple as seeing a movie into a competition over who saw it first. Susan was either brazen or oblivious enough to predate her first encounter with x, or y, right in front of the person whose experience she was, in effect, devaluing as belated. For a long time, until I recognized it as a symptom of an awesome will to power, I considered this a harmless quirk of someone who wished to be seen as generous and bestowing, or, at worst, a jump ahead of anyone else. Because she was—often—astonishingly generous.

Yet the strongest feelings I associate with her are anger, contempt, and resentment. It was as if she reserved her positive emotions for works of art, and to a lesser extent their creators, and for people in distress at least six thousand miles away from her usual surroundings. She played the role of neighbor much less charitably than that of world citizen. The contents of daily reality exasperated her beyond endurance. She was unflaggingly rude to waiters, cab drivers, hotel clerks. After she was recognized by a diner cashier we'd bought sandwiches from, her displeasure was frightening. "He only knew who I was because he saw me on *television*," she said disgustedly, as if unmasking a former concentration camp guard.

Reality is, for the most part, a great disappointment. Susan took it as a personal insult.

It feels improbable, but eight years have already passed since she died. A few months ago, as J. and I boarded a flight for Oslo, I remembered something from 1985 or 1986: I was often in touch with Hans Magnus Enzensberger, who told me he had run into Susan at a Houston literary conference.

"She must be cross with me about something," he said. "We took the same flight to New York, and when I waved to her she ignored me."

A short time later, Susan was bagging unwanted books to sell at the Strand. Kathy Acker had asked me to give Susan her then self-published novels. Thinking it was probably not a good idea, I had. I now noticed them at the top of the pile.

"Can you believe this person," Susan said, plucking up

a small book with a green cover and waving it with distaste. "She actually writes, 'Dear Susan Sontag, Please write about my books and make me famous.' This woman is a friend of yours?"

There was absolutely no way to defend someone like Kathy to someone like Susan. For one thing, they lived ten blocks from each other. If Kathy had been Croatian or from Micronesia, then perhaps . . . The moment passed, as moments do. I mentioned talking to Magnus. Susan's back went up. She inhaled noisily, a bull about to charge, as she did when unspeakable things wafted into her ken.

"Last week," she said, "I waved at him when I was getting on the same plane. He turned his back on me and acted like I wasn't there."

"That's so funny! He told me he did wave to you, and you didn't wave back. Maybe you didn't see him waving," I suggested, "and then when you waved, he was looking the other way."

It sounded reasonable, but that was the problem. Susan wasn't having it.

"He's a *liar*," she said, with startling violence.

It occurs to me now that Magnus probably upgraded his cheap conference ticket to first class, while Susan had to sit in coach. She had no money at the time except whatever Roger Straus gave her. A German national treasure (and quite an entrepreneurial one), Magnus has been rich since the 1960s. Susan considered herself a national monument, but had the misfortune to live in a country that cares less about intellectuals than it does about the ash content of dog food. I can't swear that this had anything to do with her animus against Enzensberger. It might have. She may have had other reasons for calling him a liar, for all I know. She never mentioned any.

★

After my breakfast amphetamine and tepid instant Nescafé on Monday mornings, I maneuvered into light Santa Monica Boulevard traffic and headed for the 101, *The Rise and Fall of Ziggy Stardust and the Spiders from Mars* on the eight-track player. Mild cases of road rage and games of chicken in the lanes around me brought the earth plane into reach as speed dissolved my hangover into soothing oneness with the ozone-heavy smog. *Goddamn it*, I sometimes thought, *I am doing something noble with my nonexistence, even if it's something small and stupid that anyone could do.*

Breezing into reception at Legal Aid instantly sucked me into the Problem of Race in America. Greeted by incredulous, angry stares, my blood pressure surged with selfless virtue. The loathing "our clients" directed at homosexuals was thought to derive from indoctrination by the black churches. Relieving their distress while meeting their hostility with a smile, I habitually mistook my reciprocal loathing of them for righteous anger over the racially motivated injustices that they sat in the waiting room glowering about.

These unfortunate souls had usually been served with papers from landlords, warrants from the sheriff's office, notices of repossession and imminent seizure of goods, intimidating documents that demanded an immediate, legally framed reply. By the time people showed up at Legal Aid, the last possible deadline for this response had usually long passed, and the remaining available recourse was practically nil. It was always the eleventh hour, or considerably later. All the business of our office was a rushed, urgent, desperate last-ditch effort. Overtime was the only time we knew.

The clients came in all shapes and sizes, though they tended to be either gaunt and indignant or fat and tearful. They were victims of domestic violence. Also perpetrators of domestic violence. Their husbands or wives or children were serving time for assault, drug dealing, car theft, arson, kidnapping their own children, or petty larceny. They ran amok in supermarkets with machetes. They walked off psychiatric wards against medical advice. They used public transit as a toilet.

Their hopelessness scared me. Yet I was fascinated by them, and hoped I was gleaning material for the novel I would write one day, if I ever worked up the nerve. Tireless raconteurs, as hopeless people tend to be, they spilled their entire lives while I shamelessly babbled encouragement while doing "intake":

"Let's see. It says here your name is Queen Elizabeth Jones? And you were in Sybil Brand for three years? Queen Elizabeth, can you tell me what you were in Sybil Brand for exactly?"

"I hit my old man."

"Uh-huh. You hit your husband."

"Nigger ain't my husband. Boyfriend smacked me, I hit him with a piece of metal."

"Wait, you got three years for hitting your boyfriend with a piece of metal?"

"Yeah, out of the mouf of a .44!"

I felt less fucked up the more I listened to them. On a good day, I considered myself lucky to have a job and a paycheck, relieved that I was only gay and unstable instead of black and penniless. I would never get arrested for stealing pickles from a Safeway. Rats would never fall into my children's breakfast cereal. I suspected nobody would

GARY INDIANA 125

ever love me enough to hit me with a piece of metal, either, but you can't have everything.

Elena, my boss, was prominent in poverty law, a ferocious advocate for the downtrodden. And more importantly for me, a narcoleptic with an endless, legal supply of pharmaceutical amphetamine. Her Eskatrol-induced mood swings were legendary in the legal field throughout California. She flipped from lunar exuberance to murderous rage in seconds, often using the latter to professional advantage.

My desk was an ideal listening post to monitor Elena's calls to adversaries in litigation: "You can tell that cunt if she files another postponement I'll come up there and *rip her uterus out through her nostrils.*" The unlimited aggression Elena poured into the phone prepared anybody in hearing range for the possibility of an actual shooting rampage as soon as she hung up. It seemed entirely possible that she had an arsenal of automatic weapons stored under the vast piles of unsorted papers stacked in her office. But the minute she got off the phone, usually, she cackled at her own amazing nerve and stayed in a speed-bright mood for several hours.

The office was a cesspit of seething racial animosities, more or less the inverted version of what prevailed outside its walls. Except for a trainee named Byron, Elena and I were the only white people within miles. Despite our habitual deference to the overwhelmingly African-American staff, which included several ex-Black Panthers, most of them hated us. "You white people" might as well have been our job titles, since practically all conversation started with it.

"You white people go home to your mansions in Bel Air, while the black man has to pick food out of garbage."

"You white people just can't see why the black man

burns his own house down. As if the black man had any option."

At a staff meeting, when I mentioned my sadness over the recent accidental death of Bubbles, a hippopotamus who'd escaped the LA zoo, this was greeted with a chorus of malicious jeers:

"You white people care more about a goddamn hippopotamus than you care about the black man."

"Poor Bubbles this, they did that to poor Bubbles . . ."

"That Bubbles ain't shit!"

All we thought about at work was food. Speed had the paradoxical effect of making us constantly hungry. It was impossible to find any food in Watts. The only safe place we could venture for lunch was the cafeteria at Martin Luther King Jr. Hospital, itself a minefield of racial animus. We contemplated bringing our own chicken from Ralph's to a place that advertised "You Buy, We Fry," then realized we would be asking for trouble. The Black Muslims ran a stand selling fried things at the end of our driveway, but, despite their complimentary copies of *Muhammad Speaks*, I stopped ordering there after they served me a hoagie full of uncooked trout.

A claque at the office threw off their slave names and rechristened themselves after African royalty: Asali, Lumumba, Masamba. Kwanzaa replaced Xmas, providing an occasion for the ex-slaves to parade around in dashikis and tribal headdresses. Many had failed the bar exam and relied on Elena to rewrite their legal briefs or handle their court cases. They had no use for me whatever, glaring in murderous silence if I asked to borrow a staple gun.

A daunting bunch. Most of the cases involved evictions. Most of our clients' landlords were Jewish. The former slaves viewed Jews as parasitic vermin, and all whites as obviously Jewish. Lumumba Jones, a dead ringer for Papa Doc of Haiti, sometimes hissed, *"You forgot your yarmulke,"* when I came through the door in the morning. *"You forgot your spear and the bone in your nos*e," I snapped back at him one bleary morning, which would have occasioned a star-chamber staff conference if a disgruntled client hadn't phoned in a bomb threat a few minutes later.

Whether fearless by nature or just constantly speeding, Elena labored for hours at the office after closing time. In exchange for Eskatrol, I did, too. Watts turned scary after dark. Actually it was scary all the time. The unlighted parking lot looked like an engraved invitation to Jack the Ripper.

I was atrocious at filing and typing. I lost important documents and forgot phone messages. I spent whole days writing never-to-be-finished novels and fooling with my hair. No one minded. Absolutely nobody wanted to work in Watts. The fact that I was willing to made me invaluable.

Nothing truly dire ever happened to me—except once, coming off the 101, when a stray bullet whizzed through my windshield and exited the rear window, leaving me with a mouthful of shattered glass—though people were constantly getting shot or stabbed or assaulted with lead pipes or brained with weed whackers in the neighborhoods around the office. The shootout that turned the Symbionese Liberation Army into French fries had happened only twenty blocks north of our office the year before. As soon as I exited the freeway, an atmosphere of gathering mayhem seeped into the car like Dickensian fog. The streets had a look of feral abandonment, of machine guns concealed in baby carriages, of knifing massacres at backyard barbecues.

If I hadn't been high all the time, I would've been petrified. Instead I felt fatalistic and pretended things would work out fine.

I was irritated that Veruschka told a journalist friend the story about the rat. Although I had heard it from somebody else, I thought of it as my story and wanted to use it before everyone in the world heard it.

"I'll tell you a better story," she said. "A famous soccer player became very depressed and one day he threw himself in front of a bus. The driver of the bus was a big fan of the soccer player. When he found out that he had accidentally killed his idol, he went into a depression and jumped off the roof of a building. Then the bus driver's wife became depressed. She went to a psychiatrist, but her life was ruined so she swallowed an overdose of pills. The psychiatrist felt like a total failure when he heard about this and hanged himself in his office."

"How much of this is true?"

"Maybe none of it is true, but it's a better story, isn't it?"

eight

Mastiu reminds me of a sailor in a Cocteau drawing, hair cropped to his skull, rippling muscles, exaggeratedly full lips, thick fingers, his heavy penis half-aroused in his cargo pants when he steps off the elevator every day at one o'clock, or two, a creature with animal grace and a holy stupidity eager to be kissed and fondled, petted and fussed over like a child. His lubricious joy is obvious and lovely, but a little strange. Why should he like me?

A yellow legal pad records our messy attempts, when other things fail, to communicate more than the primitive understandings we already have, which only require blunt gestures for eating, drinking, or the other thing. These efforts all end in uncertainty, however literal, specific, and simpleminded we both try to be.

If there is any space left on a page, Mastiu stops my pencil from starting a new one, even if the current sheet suggests an exit-less garden maze, or the chalkboard pentimento of multiple revised algebra equations, my semi-phonetic Spanish overlapping his labored scrawls and the crossed-out words his deafness confuses with similar-sounding ones, an alphabetic folie à deux of limitless futility. He definitely understands the world completely differently than I do.

Several nights ago I ran into his friend from the French

café. She stood on the mobbed sidewalk beside the Bim Bom, still wearing her faux-leather jacket, her chin bobbing, her mouth open in silent laughter. It took a minute or two to perceive that several young men surrounding her were deaf-mutes.

She never offered her name, and didn't name the *sordomudos* she introduced with perfunctory gestures. I watched them signing, telling one another unguessable things that appeared finely nuanced and at the same time simple, devoid of abstraction. On nights that followed, I became aware that an improbably large percentage of the crowd consisted of other deaf-mutes—male, female, young, middle-aged, old, scattered through the crush, chatting and signaling *en passant* with their hands while mingled with the general chaos.

Mastiu showed up at Bim Bom last night. I had never seen him there before. I was sitting with five particular *sordomudos*, who by then had started to collect around me whenever I showed up, expecting me to treat them to drinks, give them cigarettes, and pay them exclusive attention. It was becoming obnoxious.

Mastiu half-lifted me from the table and clamped me in an unmistakable embrace of total ownership. This led to a lot of deaf-mute conversation between Mastiu and the others, most of it visibly about me, and brainlessly vulgar on the part of my recently acquired friends. Cubans with all their faculties are frank and casual when discussing sex, but this torrent of deaf-mute innuendo was something different, with a nasty, sordid edge that made Mastiu look as uncomfortable as I felt—though the fact that he engaged with it at all disgusted me. I had no way of disrupting it. What I would have liked to communicate at that juncture was too complicated to get across. Within their own realm, the deaf-mutes are streetwise and clever. But from outside, in the world of sound and speech, they seemed obdurately stupid and boorish. This had to do, I realized, with how these particular deaf-mutes had been raised, by the poorest of the poor down here—feral children, basically. Whatever schools and social services exist for them are probably alienating, if they're anything like the Young Pioneers or Junior Communist League or whatever indoctrinating clubs normal children get processed through. Still, even the outright thugs I know on this island have better manners and more respect for other people's boundaries than these Bim Bom *sordomudos*. (If Ferd were here, having these thoughts, he would be in a paroxysm of guilt by now. But I want to understand this as it is, not how it should be.)

In the hour we stayed there, I saw that Mastiu has little interest in using any language beyond the necessary minimum, even a language he evidently uses quite eloquently, keeping other deaf-mutes hanging, so to speak, on his every word. I also noted the difference between his open, provincial manner and the cringing, sneaky vibe of the city *sordomudos*, who give off the aura of a criminal gang, and act like conspirators whenever a non-handicapped person is around. I should feel sorry for them, and I don't somehow, which should make me feel guilty, and it doesn't.

Mastiu and I finally walked away and bought some plastic cups from a girl who sells them in front of the gas station, where we bought a pint of rum and some cans of tuKola. (It costs a dollar less than real Coca-Cola, and I can't tell the difference.) Then we crossed the highway to the Malecón, where some boys I knew were sitting on the sea wall. Mastiu kept beaming idiotically as if he'd won a prize. At the apartment later, he let me know that he absolutely hated the Bim Bom. He made the universal "blabbermouth" gesture to say the Bim Bom people talked too much.

He lives off the island's tenuous grid, earning chump change with a fishing rod, at night, on some obscure marsh or faraway beach. He isn't scheming for a better life, or emigration. I doubt if Mastiu has ever heard of Karl Marx, or has the remotest idea what communism is. I'd be surprised if even José Martí stirs any patriotic fervor in his loins. His capacity for abstraction is nil. He's an unassimilable person. They're found in any society, eliciting honorary compassion, inspiring feeble remedial efforts, basically left alone to their own unimaginable devices.

The two or three afternoon hours we spend together give mornings a definite form (breakfast, writing) and leave an aftermath of fucked-out, languid indirection. Once he's been here, I find it impossible to return to any memory I've been trying to recover. Instead I replay the previous hour's porn movie with a view to improving it when we reshoot it the next day.

I worry at times that he'll disappear and meet a harsh fate I'll never hear about. Even with Cubans who can speak and hear, it's hard to maintain continuity, as my Spanish is tentative and imprecise, and no one I know here has more than perfunctory English. It's usually true that if people want to find you in Havana, they will. But if you want to find them, it isn't so simple. People do vanish. They get sent back to their provinces by police, or get swallowed by some desperate enterprise that takes them out of the city or lands them in prison. Is this some kind of love, I wonder, and if it is, does it really have anything to do with me?

★

With its seedy desuetude of a James M. Cain novel, the Bryson Apartments exuded nostalgia for a previous Los Angeles. It was owned by Fred MacMurray, a well-guarded secret that enhanced its atmosphere of *Double Indemnity*. Famed long ago as a warren of love nests rented by studio executives for their starlet mistresses, the ten-story Beaux-Arts heap was one of several derelict follies in the triangular ghost town between Lafayette and MacArthur Parks: the Wilshire Royale, the Asbury, and the Park Plaza, also known as the Elks Building. The Royale had a street-side coffee shop with black glass windows. A block farther east on Wilshire, a revival cinema never drew a single customer, a few doors from a Mexican restaurant that featured an anemic mariachi band serenading an empty dining room.

It was a perfect neighborhood for hiding away from the world and pretending time had stopped. The Wilshire District belonged to a forgotten era. The fourth-floor apartment came furnished, with king-size bed and chintz-covered sofa and a fold-out dining table with chairs. A glass-paneled breakfront. Thin gray carpeting wall to wall. A pleasantly flimsy set for Kraft Television Theatre, circa 1956. It had a Hollywood bathroom with black-and-white tiles, an efficiency kitchen stocked with plates and pans and a look of deluded 1930s optimism. A square balcony protruded over Wilshire Boulevard like a giant flowerbox. Side windows over Rampart Street faced the Royale, perennially stalled under renovation and vacant except for the street-level coffee shop, with a handful of elderly tenants in forty-watt rooms, shuffling behind half-drawn shades in sad gray underwear or staring down at the street waiting to die.

The Bryson was haunted by myriad ghosts, among whom I numbered Stephanie, a spectral, transsexual night clerk, whose estrogen storms produced theatrical mood swings that made her conversation impossibly self-

referential and confusing. Everyone living in the Bryson
suffered from insomnia, I discovered. They wandered the
halls after midnight looking lost, or knocked on random
doors to "borrow" cigarettes or recount their latest dreams
to strangers. In daylight, the Bryson ceased to exist. I never
saw another tenant leave for work in the morning or come
home at night.

Many tenants, for legal or technical reasons, couldn't
operate a motor vehicle, and turned up at my door at weird
hours to hustle rides, sometimes to an all-night diner on
Miracle Mile. Another popular destination was the Ralphs
market on Sixth Street. I made the mistake of ferrying a
frowzy, unlovely couple named Joni and Hank to Ralphs
several times, creating the false impression that I enjoyed
their company. They described themselves as sex addicts.
Soon they considered me their friend. They began
suggesting nauseating three-ways while piling giant bags
of Cheez Doodles and cases of Coca-Cola into their
shopping cart. They had a trailer-park greasiness I
associated with Charles Manson. Joni and Hank's dream
was to "break into show business," a dream so remote
from plausibility that it might have been touching, if they
had been less needy and mentally dim.

An obese girl named Martha lived on the seventh floor
with her mother, Eleanor, in a flat empty of furniture except
for the bed they shared. Their place was a four-handed
handicraft factory where they crafted little elfin effigies
and novelty pins for curio shops in what remained of old
downtown LA. Martha and Eleanor had been swindled,
they claimed, on a goose-shaped lamp they'd designed
that I saw all over the city in those days. Each blamed the
other for selling the patent, which occupied the place in
their reveries that Belle Reve had in Blanche DuBois's.

They were at each other's throats day and night. Martha was not young, but never having lived apart from her mother, had frozen at the emotional age of puberty.

Eleanor desperately wanted to get Martha married off. She was a kindly, self-interested shrew. She saw any male they met as husband material. Martha developed an insensible, elephantine crush on me, and a fantasy that we shared a stormy romantic bond. She poured unnerving histrionics into our glancing encounters, invented "dates" she accused me of breaking. She began letting herself into my apartment—I often forgot to lock up—as if we lived together. It took more tact and patience than I had to get rid of her. Her passion ended one evening when she barged in to find a recently paroled car thief sprawled on my living room sofa, stroking his enormous prick.

Martha decided I had "jilted" her, and never spoke to me again.

Enzensberger writes of a train passenger who feels lucky to have a whole compartment to himself. A second passenger enters. The first one resents him for ruining his luck. When a third passenger arrives, the first two bond in silent hostility against the intruder. The third passenger mentally aligns himself with the other two in resentment against a fourth passenger who shows up, and so on.

The opposite happens at a roulette table. The gamblers welcome the arrival of new players. As the wheel spins they form an excited family. They buy each other extra drinks, tell stories, joke. They're thrilled when anybody at the table wins. They share gambling systems and superstitions, talk about their jobs, even exchange business cards, though it's understood that what starts in a casino ends in a casino. When they lose, they don't care. When players leave the table, they're sad.

One night I had won six thousand dollars by two in the morning. Everybody thought it was hilarious that I kept winning. Until four, the table was crowded. Then one player left. Then another. By five, I sat alone with ten thousand dollars in chips stacked in front of me. I felt abandoned and horrible. I put the whole pile on double zero, which absolutely never comes up. The croupier understood my relief when I lost everything.

nine

I paid a peso and took the *lancha* across the port to Regla.
The ferry landing and the boats are disintegrating from
gravity and oxidation. The passengers looked relieved to
get out of central Havana. Some carried bicycles. A few
women held babies to their chests. One grizzled man sat
on a bulkhead and smoked a thin cigar. The boat churned
up orange peels and plastic soda bottles in the brackish
water. We crossed several historical time zones in the space
of a nautical mile.

The notable things in Regla are the Belot refinery and
the Galainela shipyard, and a massive electricity plant
from the 1930s. Regla people are said to be fiercely loyal
to the Revolution. In Regla itself, no house or other
building, nothing worn or driven or purchased in one of
the darkened shops, appears to date from later than 1959.
Regla is a center of Santeria and other voodoo. Every
shabby residence, however small, has a shrine room heaped
with flowers, candles, saucers of chicken blood and gris-
gris, where people sacrifice poultry to the Black Virgin
and cast spells on enemies, cure malignant tumors, obtain
winning lottery numbers.

Old women smoked cigars in doorways. School kids in
blue-and-white uniforms skipped along a potholed main
street. Horse-drawn wagons clobbered down alleys of dried

mud. The world slowed down, de-mechanized suddenly, like Algiers when you cross from New Orleans, or Montevideo from Buenos Aires. People moved differently. They were striking to look at, sensuous as figured textiles but spectral and impervious to outsiders, like the projections in *The Invention of Morel*.

The stillness reminded me of New Hampshire summers, before the forests bordering Derry were razed for tract developments. The landscape of secret places, fallow orchards, and forgotten graveyards, all vanished now under golf courses and malls. Time passed like slow-pouring syrup. I don't think it will be long after I'm dead that nature won't exist. The world will be a throbbing hive of computer chips.

Lately, at two p.m. I drift into sleep, no matter what I'm doing. I fall asleep in taxis, sitting on park benches, anywhere at all. This happened before, in Mexico. It turned out that I was deathly ill. I can't worry about that. If I die, fine. It would be lovely to die in my sleep, too relaxed and tired to resist the final exit. The *siesta* is not a Cuban habit, but there is a space in the *media tarde* when nothing occurs and the world might as well be in a trance. The best place at that hour is the Hotel Colina patio, or the cement park above the landing stage in Casablanca, where the other *lancha* crosses the harbor.

I walked the length of a heavily scarred, inclined street, the perfunctory sidewalk broken like the wake of an iceberg cutter. The road intersected a square where the *iglesia* of the Black Virgin stood dozing in the heat. Boys in the square had abandoned their soccer game to try on each other's jerseys. Two police looked asleep on their feet. A woman in a green skirt paced back and forth, her lips moving as she read something on a clipboard.

A movie theater. What might have been a dance hall forty years ago behind the scaling columns of an arcade. A pastry shop. Stores that looked closed but had people inside. A car. A water truck. The air smelled fresher than Havana, but there was no breeze. The palms looked set in bronze. Calm, slightly dead, with the eternal stillness of a parking lot in the Mojave.

You would never find foreigners there, except on a bus tour. There is nothing to see in Regla besides the Black Virgin. The Belot refinery was blown up during Batista days and reconstructed after Castro came. I like places where nothing happens, the time between events. I am wary of events. I do not welcome them. Events make it difficult to breathe and remind you that death is coming. Last night on the Malecón, two cheerful guys from Guantánamo urged me to visit them there. "Everything is really, really clean in Guantánamo," one said. "The houses, the forest, the water, all very, very clean," said the other. Havana is filthy. No doubt about it. The best-kept neighborhood has piles of filth in it somewhere. "And you will love it there, because nothing ever happens."

★

I developed a building crush on Lester, who lived across the hall at the Bryson. Lester wore the ruffled shirts and satin trousers of a Carnaby Street dandy, his hair an unraveling Brillo pad. He looked like Marc Bolan. Anyone with hair that way does. Like many junkies, Lester subsisted on uncooked hot dogs and beer, and resembled an adorable sea mammal, a baby dolphin or a manatee, exciting a protective impulse he manipulated with childlike mastery.

If Lester coveted a little object in my apartment, he

cooed over it until I gave it to him. When I happened not to, he stole it. He had a skanky allure, demanding no effort on his part. A charming creep. I wanted to corner him, disable his slippery defenses, pin him to the floor, and rape him.

I thought my fantasies about Lester might finally be going somewhere one night when he came over and asked suggestively if I would answer a personal question.

"Sure, why not?"

"Okay, I was wondering. Have you ever had sex with a dead person?"

I assumed a blasé expression. It crossed my mind that the dead person in question might be Lester's idea of himself, but it seemed that a mate of his working for a mortician was having fun with bodies he embalmed and had offered to let Lester in on the action.

"I think it's against the law," I said.

"Yeah, right," Lester said. "But I mean, what isn't?"

For a moment, I imagined the question of his sexual preference resolved: unless a decedent's penis were frozen upright in rigor mortis, sex with a male corpse would hardly be worthwhile. Lester undoubtedly had a dead vagina in mind. But I then considered that you could, in a pinch, fuck a dead man in the ass. Anyway, most people I knew at this time weren't picky about the gender of their sexual partners. Maybe Lester went either way. I prodded him to narrow things down. He was too stoned to focus on what I was saying.

"It sounds extreme, but it really wouldn't be hurting anybody. There's nobody home. I'm repulsed by the idea, but I also gotta admit, I'm kind of fascinated in a sick way. Guy works for a funeral home in Palmdale. I'm not asking for advice. I just wondered if . . ."

Lester's voice went all drifty. "Nah, never mind. Forget I brought it up."

"No, Lester, go ahead, this is interesting."

He rubbed his oily nose and gnawed his lip.

"Well, say some night I . . . need a ride out to Palmdale, would you give me a lift?"

A ballroom on the tenth floor crowned the building. It hadn't been used since the 1940s. Carved cherrywood chairs ranged along the walls. A carpet of dust on the parquet floor hadn't registered a single footprint in thirty years. A tiered chandelier missing most of its crystals hung from an Arabic ceiling rotten with wood lice.

A phantom ball swirled through this cavernous, forgotten space, where I never saw another living soul. Ghosts, yes, all the ghosts of the hotel had migrated up there over the decades. The parquet tiles, the moth-eaten velvet walls, the decomposing ceiling beams were all imprinted with spirits of the great long ago. The window glass along all four walls had fallen out. I'd discovered an inviolable, secret place with the wind blowing through it, high above the world.

Across from my hotel balcony in Istanbul, on the top floor of a three-story yellow house, a man whose head I've never seen is lying on a duvet, naked except for black socks and white underpants, channel-flipping a TV with the remote held in a milky hand in gray darkness. I can't see how old he is or anything else about him. His sprawled flesh suggests someone who has given up and decided to live in his underpants for the rest of his life, a hibernating animal living off stored body fat. I can't really tell if he is fat, or if the faint light catching his body from the streetlamp makes him appear bloated and blubbery.

ten

Mastiu is an encyclopedia of carnal knowledge, but this is the only knowledge I glean from him. The better I learn his body's tastes and textures, the greater a puzzle the person inside it becomes. Sometimes he's a baby in a grown-up's body, or a schoolboy who barely knows the alphabet. Sitting close together on the terrace, we decorate yellow legal pads with pencil threads of broken Spanish. A sad suspicion that his brain is damaged seems belied by flashes of rakish cunning that appear at the corners of his mouth, or when he flares his nostrils at some remark I expect to fly over his head, casting the question into doubt again. Glimmers of intelligence in his personality hint at some undiscovered secret person he becomes when he isn't with me. But basically, I think, he isn't that bright.

He enslaves me with his cock and loves me into submission with the bullish thrustings of a steam shovel. He isn't brutal, exactly, just implacable. I could even say he's a sensitive lover, but only because he never really hurts me. I'm aware the whole time how much stronger and more substantial his body is, and that his need has total priority: he doesn't even notice if I come or not. To be fair about it, that isn't my priority either.

It's so much a complete pornographic fantasy, though, so consummate and flawless it can't possibly go on for

many days before reality steps in to spoil it. Since when
does life give you what you want without fucking it up as
soon as possible? Okay: For now, today, in some drastically
limited but gratifying sense, I have exactly what I want.
He can't hear anything I say, I don't have to listen to him
talking, we don't even have the means most people have at
their disposal to ruin each other. It's how I want it, so I
tell myself: he's the man, he fucks me good, I can have his
cock in me as much as I want, and that's all he wants,
more or less. When he's back in his pants he turns into a
puppy. Perfect.

Puppies are adorable, but they don't have fascinating
inner lives. Before his awkwardly held pencil completes a
word on the yellow paper he scratches out the erratic
lettering and starts over. His difficulty printing revives my
downward estimate of his IQ. I lose interest in his clumsy
list of bodies of water where he fishes, a dreary penmanship

exercise that doesn't interest him, either. I can do fine without conversation. It's these dutiful attempts at having one that begin to bore me.

In a gloomy hour of the morning, days ago, I understood that if I knew for certain that Mastiu is "challenged," I would ignore my qualms about sleeping with him. This realization makes me queasy every day when he leaves. Of course I feel something's wrong, and knowing I'm capable of deliberately doing what I think is wrong—capable of planning to do the same wrong thing again and again—is really damning. All right. "I'll own it," as idiotic people say these days. I won't add lying to myself to the disgrace of exploiting the mentally challenged.

But I'm honestly not sure if he is. He could be slightly retarded and mimicking a normal adult when he acts like one, but as plausibly fully cognizant, his vocal noises making him sound "slow." He won't teach me sign language. I read and write Spanish poorly. It's probable Mastiu wasn't taught anything beyond a third-grade level. That's not unusual among deaf-mutes here, who all seem a bit stupid to someone with full sensory equipment, though they're street-smart—within a small cluster of streets, but all the same.

Anyway, he picked me up, not the other way around. I'm not corrupting an innocent. He's twenty-three. He's been married, or says he has. He's fathered a child. That I believe without question. He's been boning both sexes in record numbers since the age of twelve, so I'm hardly the first, though that doesn't really make anything else I can think of all right.

We go on scribbling misspellings on the yellow paper before and after sex, a labored, thin communication that turns ridiculous when I hazard any lengthy message involving a passage of time: past, present, and future are the same to him. I tried to describe my ferry trip. He interpreted my crude drawing of a boat and the harbor, replete with arrows and a lighthouse, to mean I'm soon going far away by ship.

Two or three hours groping for words of one syllable are all I can handle. Drinks, if he wants drinks. He can make Neyda's off-putting lunch disappear if he likes. He scowls when he sniffs the plate, but gobbles everything down in twenty seconds.

Mastiu cares about eating, fucking, and catching a peso cab back to Cotorro instead of the bus, with some leftover change in his pocket. Fine with me, if he's nice about it. Not every old whore gets swived to smithereens by a twenty-three-year old on a daily basis. But he's also tiresome. His fishing job finishes up soon and it won't be heartbreaking when he leaves, I don't think.

He knows I'm at Bim Bom at night picking up other men. Some of them have known me forever and think it a treat to get trashed on my balcony and bang me once a year for old time's sake. The other deaf-mutes tell Mastiu whom I talk to, hoping he'll strangle me in a jealous rage: six or seven of them gang around, whipping up dramas on the waterfront with sign language, more importunate and in-my-face every time they spot me. I really don't see myself as Desdemona. Mastiu doesn't care who I sleep with, as long as it's not one of them. But really I'm tired of them all, including him.

Last week, offering what he takes for granted as my swooning dream, he indicated that he was spending the night. He rested his cheek on an imaginary pillow to demonstrate this. The whole thing was farcical. For one thing he didn't ask, and I had other plans. I didn't want to sleep when he did. I felt like drinking on the terrace and going down to feed the cats. He grew insistent, finally pushy. As soon as we got under the sheets, his cell phone vibrated and lit up with text messages, on what looked suspiciously like cue. Fresh messages beamed and gurgled in the dark every few minutes. He tapped out replies instantly—curious, no hearing or spelling problems there— and sank under the sheets. Between calls he thrashed around until all the bedding coiled around him, making restive noises that were building up to the revelation that he had to leave, supposedly to deal with whatever the texts were about, hoping I'd believe he didn't want to go.

Such a drag. I hate being taken for a fool, especially by somebody who probably is one. My eyes adjusted to the dark. I picked out the dresser, the chair where his light pants were folded, the giant mirror on the wall, the murky shapes reflected in it. A little after midnight. It was pathetically obvious that the phone business had been planned with a friend, maybe the skinny girl from the French café.

However I will myself to feel about him, this is never going to be more than a client relationship. Personable, sweet, easy, as most such relationships are in Havana, but even if the verbal part of it were nuanced enough to tell him I don't want it any more complicated than it is already, and don't yearn to hear him snoring beside me, and don't care to wake up next to him or anyone else, he'd still assume what any self-respecting coquette or man-child would: "He's lying, he wants me fucking his brains out all night, it's all he thinks about. He's crazy about me."

We forget, since we'd rather not know, that everybody has his own agenda. Everybody.

The next day, he appeared at the usual dot of two. He performed an arduous pantomine assuring me that soon he'd keep his undesired promise to sleep here. After the lame charades of the night before, I completely lost patience and hustled him out to the street right after we finished the business end of the afternoon. Maybe I'll dump him altogether this week. Life's too short.

★

The Rusty Nail, West Hollywood, 1976. I drink a vodka tonic and peer out at a plate-glass window at Santa Monica Boulevard, provisionally waiting for Dane, who said he might come here, and provisionally cruising the bar for a backup, in case he doesn't show. The crimson stars of passing taillights trail across the window. The reflection of something familiar in the glass makes me shudder. Ferd has materialized suddenly, sitting at the shiny bar counter.

I turn around. It's really him, but I have that unsettling moment of wondering who "him" is. A ruffle of short hair pokes from the brow of a beige leather cap, too *sportif* by half. He wears a striped, white sports jersey with an alligator on the tit. The un-Ferdish shirt and hat compress the last seven years into a flash card. But times have changed. From his look, I think he expected me to notice him several minutes ago. The only Ferd news I've had all this time was Carol calling me in Boston to say they got divorced. I don't know how she knew where to find me or how she got my number. Not long ago she tracked me down here in Los Angeles by telephone, too.

I tried living in Boston after being released from the place where my parents put me to finish my nervous breakdown. Boston fell within their sphere of attraction, a fateful misstep I saw in advance but also felt protected by. They were close enough to send an ambulance. I missed them, too, though the warmth I felt from a distance frosted over the minute I saw them in person. New York would have been far enough away to have a nice relationship with them over the phone, but the thought of it scared me. New York was too big, too high, too indifferent, too full of millions whose miseries New York sponged up and squeezed out over the Atlantic without even tossing in a sympathy wreath.

Boston. A mean, provincial town with a heart of shit. If you looked gay to some drunken mick from Southie or walked down the wrong street at the wrong hour, you could count on an ugly reception, and maybe get beaten to a pulp or your head bashed in with a crowbar. The supposedly better element of Boston consisted of would-be bohemians floundering cluelessly in the fantasy that they lived in a cradle of civilization. As cities go, a ripe outhouse.

I got out of there as fast as possible, when someone offered me a Legal Aid job in LA. Not the one in Watts, but an earlier paralegal slot at the central office on Eighth Street. The Eighth Street office sat in a dead zone where Bunker Hill had been demolished that looked as desolate and nearly as scary as Watts. I didn't miss Eighth Street later on, though we had been able to buy good sandwiches at Langer's instead of skipping lunch or risking our lives foraging for food.

LA in the 1970s was a sleepy backwater, which no one born around that time or afterward ever believes, but it's true. Asked to point out evidence of LA's defensively touted cultural bounty at the time, one of the lawyers I worked for cited Hamburger Hamlet. All the same, Boston was the anus of the USA by comparison. After settling at the Bryson, I felt less at war with myself than I had in my entire life. I felt like a grown-up. I felt almost home. And now here was Ferd.

Passing time had bleached them into unreality, but the last days in San Francisco persisted in a faint phosphorescent residue of anger about being used like a Kleenex. This emitted its dying glow as I went over to the bar. I made a snide, lame crack about people who eat people being the lousiest people in the world, which made him wince and pull himself back slightly, as if expecting a full barrage. But a real display of hostility didn't seem justified, since I no longer actually felt any.

I've had spotty images of Broderick Street available for viewing in my head since 1969. I've never kept them in sight long enough to discover what I think about them. Forcing them to mean something has never appealed to me, though I've written about them here, so I suppose now I have. It seemed prudent not to bring any of it up, but inevitably we did talk about it that night, and never spoke of it again. Ferd had given Broderick Street a lot of reflection. He confessed to feeling guilty about that whole period. He told me he felt responsible for the rape, which I felt was really taking it too far.

I had never figured out what to feel about getting raped. Men were not supposed to be raped, and when it happened, nobody called it that. If you were male you were supposed to be immune to it, or strong and scrappy enough that nobody could really penetrate you without your cooperation. In my mind, the incident in San Francisco resembled the cemetery acid trip in *Easy Rider*, and it made me sad. But weird as it sounds, the fact is that I was raped a second time, by a male nurse, in the place where they put me after I flew home from San Francisco.

Two rapes seemed more ridiculous than tragic. Perhaps this sounds glib. But prevailing opinion that what happened to me was not even possible forced me to suck it up and keep my mouth shut about it. As it happens, I reported the second rape, with the consequence that the psychiatrist assigned to me filed an affidavit swearing I had admitted fantasizing the whole thing, while the hospital administration quietly transferred the rapist to a job at a different facility.

After the second sexual assault that I was supposed to feel less manly about having been the recipient of, turning both events into an ugly comedy was the only way I could deal with them. Anyway, it sounded as if Ferd, for all his sophistication, had cast himself as the agonized father who didn't protect me from the Hells Angels in a script written for afternoon television.

"You know something," I said when he finished flagellating himself, "I wasn't as traumatized as you seem to think I was."

I hear his voice again, which I can't really describe. He

had a very individual voice. A slightly droning one, crackly, with high-pitched, piping inflections. Its ever-mysterious, hypnotic effect on the evening in question revived that fierce, familial, occult recognition of who we really were in the core of our souls.

"Really?" The slightly sunken, drooping eyelids that gave him his Baudelairean aura flipped up in surprise.

"Oh, go ahead, asshole, you were about to say what a relief it is to hear it when you realized what that would sound like."

I'm not sure whether we saw Dane that night. I can't exactly locate a free-floating memory of us three driving to East Hollywood in Dane's exterminator truck and doing the bars. It definitely happened, but maybe on a different night. Of the night at the Rusty Nail, I only clearly remember the beginning of a long conversation that continued somewhere or other until closing time, stiffly at first but then sloppy with alcohol and an excess of drunken feeling. We weren't the same people anymore. Ferd hadn't injected heroin in years. I took speed, but only to get through insanely many hours of work and cruising bars after work and a lot of fucking after the bars. Chronic sleep deprivation was causing me to go numb all the time and forget things, but being numb agreed with me and I had nothing important to remember at the time. I was up all the time, but never really high.

After seven years, Ferd and I had no sexual or romantic interest in each other at all. Yet there was an unexpectedly strong connection. In our different ways, we had been thinking about the same things, reading more or less the same books, paying attention to the same awful things happening in the world.

He had finished a teaching degree in Chicago,

abandoning "the arts" after splitting up with Carol. He joined a splinter faction of the Weather Underground. After that, he migrated from one militant leftist group to another. From what I gathered, this progression reflected his growing conviction that nonviolence had stopped being a workable strategy around 1973. I had drawn a similar conclusion, though unlike Ferd, I had no intention of doing anything about it. I've never felt any burning desire to change the world—it's completely beyond my capacity. It was beyond his, too, though Ferd eventually did change part of the world for the better. (This is much more his real legacy than my personal dealings with him, I hasten to add.)

After he left San Francisco, politics really became Ferd's life. As it happens, it had also been his life before San Francisco, though I never knew this, weirdly enough, until after he died. Before I met him he had worked in the South during the darkest days of the civil rights movement, and he'd done many other really praiseworthy, selfless political things, full time. I can't account for having known precious little about his life before 1969, except by saying that no one who met him where and when I did would have imagined this history, and he never told me about it later.

This is odd, for sure, because I lived with him for months at a time, intermittently, over a twenty-year period. We spoke once or twice a week from 1987 until a few months before he died. It's just the way it was, he seldom said anything about his early life. It occurs to me that some people bring their whole histories into friendships and love affairs, out of habit, and others don't, without necessarily being secretive. It's jarring all the same, to discover that you know little about someone you consider an intimate friend.

I had taken him for a besotted aesthete and would-be

French decadent in San Francisco. Perhaps it was the heroin, but he played this role to perfection. When we met again in Los Angeles, he had shed that pose entirely. He had moved back to California, apparently, out of rigid fealty to a commune of militant, gay leftists living in a house in—Echo Park? Los Feliz?

I never visited the commune. I don't think I ever knew where it was. Ferd's description of it in the Rusty Nail made it sound like a weird cult of doctrinaire, puritanical faggots. Men joining the commune, for example, had to take oaths that they would only have sexual relations with other commune members. This was the acid test of their ideological purity, because none of them found any of the others remotely attractive in that way.

I should mention that regardless of how respectfully Ferd treated me, I felt intimidated by him. I thought he knew more than I did, particularly about political theory,

Marxism, superstructure and base, all the canonical texts of communism I found impossibly written, et cetera, et cetera. This is why, when he spoke of the gay panthers, or whatever they were, I didn't reveal how completely nuts they sounded to me. In 1976, part of me felt outraged at the lot of my Legal Aid clients—the better part of me, I think—and still believed in a violent change of the social order. Any group committed to disruption had my meaningless endorsement, although I thought it preferable that Ferd's group make the revolution without my assistance. They seemed to have more time to concentrate on it, and no appealing ideas about how to carry it off.

Another commune rule: a member was only permitted to masturbate standing before a full-length mirror. "The point," Ferd said, "is that when you actually stand there and make yourself come, you see what you're actually doing." I don't recall what he said that actually was. I'm not sure if he said masturbation was the ultimate surrender to an evil, ideological paradigm—an analysis beyond my grasp—or if this jack-off-in-a-mirror concept had to do with Lacanian analysis, or what else it could possibly be thought to illuminate. I knew better than to ask for an encore of Ferd's explanation. They had their reasons, whatever they were.

In a breathless hush, Ferd disclosed that he and his fellow communards, in concert with enclaves elsewhere in California, planned to travel later in the year to Houston, where they intended to set off an explosive device at the International Women's Conference, for ideological reasons I think Ferd explained at some hour when I was too drunk to follow them.

Well. The second chapter of my Ferd story opened, if not with a bang, at least the rumor of one. As I mentioned,

Dane may have shown up, and we all may have gone to the One Way or the Detour, unless this happened another night, I can't be certain. I couldn't say, either, whether Dane and I went home together if he did show up, though if he had we probably did, though we sometimes didn't. By that time, I appreciated the lack of complication Dane insisted on from sexual partners. Ironically, once he perceived this, he often phoned asking if I'd meet him for a drink, or dinner and a movie.

A new, subtle register in his voice let me know if he only wanted to have a drink, without the full monty afterwards, or was leaving the decision up to me, or was set on bringing me home or at least getting a blowjob in his truck. For a long time, he'd resisted (sensibly, I think) spending time with me that didn't lead directly to the bedroom if it started outside. This changed when I stopped acting like a desperate lover who couldn't get enough of him and resented his other boyfriends.

Having Ferd in my life again made LA less lonely. It still felt like a waiting room. I wanted it to be home, but never convinced myself that it could be.

It was also thrilling to feel connected to a terrorist. That was then, when terrorism made a kind of sense, though what kind I can no longer tell you.

After a suicide bombing, forensic investigators immediately "look for the face mask." The shock waves from an explosion blow the bomber's head to smithereens but for some reason leave the face intact as a peeled, rubbery pentimento of the missing person, like a condom that stares back at you. After the Benazir Bhutto assassination, they found two.

eleven

Yesterday a feeling of evil spreading everywhere like fog crept up on me. I was sitting on the patio of the Hotel Nacional near the cliff edge. The world has gotten very small, I thought. For some the world is limitless. Others find it small indeed, and finally crack from claustrophobia. I was gazing at the horizon where Florida was hidden behind the sea. The Caribbean looked stagnant, despite the tide crashing on the sea wall flinging up dramatic plumes that drenched people on the sidewalk.

A dream last night, with Kathy Acker in it: something that evaporated in layers as I woke up, full of noisy fragments, from the summer we went to the piers at night, Kathy in a sailor suit and cap, I in a silk Donna Karan blouse, white Courrèges boots, and a miniskirt, two heavily lacquered little figures in drag pretending to look for quick 'n' easy sex among the leather queens and bum boys who did it in the trucks, talking loudly the whole time about Althusser and Roland Barthes, as if sitting in a crowded restaurant. The cobbled streets smelled of blood. Three-legged shadows coupled in the dark. We were an unwelcome hazard of West Street. Our voices broke the rhythm of a dozen blowjobs. We enjoyed scaring people.

Later I remembered the PEN panel. Neither of us had any use for PEN, but we were asked to speak to an audience of émigré writers, from what was then the Eastern communist bloc. Kathy, I, and a writer I'll call Bertie Wooster—a pallid, skinny, freckled beanstalk in Farmer John overalls, in the debutante phase of a monstrous career. He'd kicked it off with an interminable first novel full of insects and adolescent overreach. He later produced a veritable library of longer, fatter books, in series, with now and then a little thing no thicker than a pamphlet, as a sorbet. There was this about Bertie Wooster, or Bertie Wooster's books: he wasn't so much a force of nature as a contented slave to graphomania, like Joyce Carol Oates. (Susan once told me that if JCO happened to finish a novel en route to the airport, she turned the last page over and immediately started writing another one.) Bertie Wooster never stopped writing, apparently. Nothing he wrote could possibly interest an adult for longer than ten minutes, yet his books, soon after the PEN panel, became, if not canonical, accepted as naturally occurring ripples in the literary pond, respectfully noted one after another in the *New York Review of Books* and other places that shaped opinions. He was, I later heard, given a push by Jean Stein.

On the panel, Bertie extolled the unfettered liberty of writers in the West. This surprised us. His then current, surpassingly fat first novel had seemed, in a confused, allegorical way, critical of the capitalist order and its insurmountable contradictions. But then, I had never finished his first novel. Neither had Kathy. Life was too short. Perhaps a volte-face in favor of free markets and Chicago School neoliberalism had been effected in the second chapter. At any rate. There was something of the high school valedictorian about him. He sounded like the spawn of a clapboard colonial in Greenwich, unscrolling an address of uplifting homilies. I'm sure he wasn't from

Greenwich. He looked like a hick.

"It falls to each successive generation to uphold the
Jeffersonian ideal—" "As Lincoln said in a time of civil
war—" "To quote George Orwell in his magnificent
allegory—"

"He's going to pull an American flag out of his ass and
fart 'The Star-Spangled Banner' in a minute," Kathy
predicted in a whisper, eyes huge with incredulity. We were
startled by this blather, which frankly seemed more
pandering to the PEN club than to the émigré writers.
Maybe PEN would give him a merit badge. Kathy and I
were not intoxicated by the ever-ringing liberty that involved,
at the time, having our books automatically trashed or
ignored by the presiding covens at the *New York Times
Book Review*, the *New York Review of Books*, and, in Kathy's
case, *Vanity Fair*. I think we assumed the wildly applauding
literary refugees did not understand what Bertie Wooster
was saying, or were being polite.

When my turn came, I offered that in spite of the disaster
of "really existing socialism," a Marxist analysis of society
remained valid. I mentioned Reagan, his war on unions,
the growing chasm between rich and poor. Kathy expressed
the idea that Capital isn't a predictive book, or a Utopian
tract, but an epic novel about economic relationships, with
industrial machinery and consumer products as the central
characters. Naively, we wanted the audience, trained
dialecticians all, to know that we knew that America is only
as much fun as Disneyland if you happen to own it. We
assumed the new arrivals already saw that.

The Eastern Bloc writers were aghast, however. They
wanted 'The Star-Spangled Banner.' Their hero was Ronald
Reagan, friend of thoughtful people everywhere. One
apoplectic Hungarian likened us to Nicolae and Elena

Ceaușescu. The cocktail reception afterwards was thinly cordial. The male writers leered at Kathy's tits. The PEN people were in puppy heaven. The panel had been "spiked with controversy." Today, the same Eastern Europeans report their disgust with America in little émigré journals published in Europe. After a couple of decades, it sank in that literature has no importance here whatsoever. Some of them even hint that they miss communism, which is taking things a little far.

Unlike most people I knew, Kathy moved often, restlessly, disappearing from the scene for years at a time, teaching at faraway colleges, living a bit larger on her trust funds elsewhere than she did in Manhattan, where she put on the poor mouth for her "bohemian" friends. At lunch one day, a fifty-dollar bill slid out of her wallet as she rummaged for a single, after an epic soliloquy about her pennilessness. "I must have saved this and forgotten all about it!" Another fifty-dollar bill then dropped from the wallet. She stuffed it back in without comment.

I have no recollection of first meeting her. One day she was a fact of life. We did readings together and commiserated about our disappointments in love. She kept a tidy record of her affairs, and dropped bits of them into her books, along with her phone conversations. Her voice shot up several decibels in public, in restaurants, and often she made plans with me while aiming her voice at other tables, elaborate plans to sail around the Greek islands or launch a magazine or collaborate on a play, plans I knew would be forgotten minutes after we parted company. She was ferociously, insultingly competitive at times. We often feuded. But the gladiator reflex of writers in the mainstream was diluted in our own little skirmishes. Ultimately we were against the same things, and up against the same clubby establishment. We were basically allies, familial in the sense that we scored points against each other in private but defended each other in public.

She wrote too much, I thought. I am generally against producing books like a point spread on a horse race. I probably have the wrong idea, since all these books go out of print eventually, and the more there are, the better one's chances of accidental rediscovery—though as a motive, I think, that one isn't very compelling.

I am reading Simenon's *The Little Man from Archangel* for the third or fourth time. A deft and wondrous novel. Simenon knew how good it was, among his many good novels. When Camus won the Nobel Prize for *L'Étranger* published the same year, Simenon said, "What, they give it to that little turd?"

It's useless to look for books in English here, but a drag to pack more than a handful, since any suitcase quadruples the weight of any book placed inside it. I brought *Corrigan* by Caroline Blackwood. Two of Roni Horn's Iceland books. *Au Bonheur des Dames* by Zola. *The Age of Napoleon* by Alistair Horne, a conservative historian as it turns out, but so what. A slim book of Tomas Tranströmer poems. And *The Idiot*, a novel I read at least once a year.

A few days ago I discovered a university bookshop at the far end of Barrio Chino. Dismal and poorly lit and industrial-looking, the usual moth-eaten propaganda, books of Fidel's and Che Guevara's speeches, volumes of Marxist economic theory, with a few readable things mixed in. I bought a Spanish translation of Sebald's *Vertigo*—not without difficulty, I had only a twenty-peso CUC, and a rudely vexed clerk had to hunt resentfully for change, in the register, in the back room, in a paper bag under the counter. She finally left the store altogether and walked

two blocks down Dragones Street to a *mercado* to break
the bill. It's a diurnal problem to break anything larger
than a five-peso note into smaller notes and coins.

I try to get my larger bills broken down as early in the
day as possible. It often proves unfeasible to buy anything
within a ten-block radius of anywhere, as nobody has
change, since nobody has money. You buy things you don't
want to reduce the amount of change the vendor has to
give you, or go without whatever it is you do want. The
banks on La Rampa and the *cambio* at the Nacional Hotel
run out of small money as quickly as taxis, restaurants,
open-air markets, and cinemas do. This city runs on pocket
change. No one in New York thinks of change as money
anymore. If a cab driver owes you six-fifty after getting a
generous tip, he'll give you back six and make unhappy
noises if you insist on getting the fifty cents. Money itself
becomes waste in a society built on waste production.

Finding Sebald was flukish. Foreign books that turn up
in Havana have the peculiarity of tidewash. On the shelves
of a sidewalk kiosk near the Capitolio, I found a biography
of Elizabeth Smart—in Cuba, I'm sure, known only to me
and whoever left this biography where someone else
snatched it up and traded it for a couple cigarettes, as the
author of *By Grand Central Station I Sat Down and Wept*.
Books in English are rare and usually garbage. People
charge ridiculous prices for them. Around the Plaza de
Armas, some of the booksellers specialize in thrillers and
spy novels that tourists read on incoming flights and
abandon in hotel rooms, which have all been through the
mill, sporting ripped covers and pages falling out. Some
were evidently dropped in bath water and put out in the
sun to dry. They charge as much as sixteen CUC for a
shitty Jack Higgins novel.

In the bookshop across from the Hotel Colina, an unlikely find: Thomas Bernhard's *Obras*, looking forlorn between a stack of economic textbooks and two late, bad novels of John Dos Passos. I don't think I want to read Bernhard in Spanish. (Weird randomness of English printed matter isn't unique to Cuba; in La Paz, a bookstore near the witches' market had two ancient paperbacks of Philip K. Dick novels and multiple copies of Edmund Wilson's *The Cold War and the Income Tax*, representing the full gamut of North American literature.)

Mastiu has moved back to Santiago. His job was a seasonal thing, and the season's over. He left an indecipherable address on a scrap of paper. I doubt if I'll see him again anytime soon, if ever. It leaves a hole in the day, but not as large a hole as I'd expected.

★

I thought of Los Angeles later as a city of false starts, first paragraphs, broken-off beginnings of things that never proceeded. I was too mired in private conflicts and contradictory wishes and the static narrative of "I, me, and more me" for a description of my world to sound different than any teenager's locked diary.

I tried to write a novel, the details of which I've long forgotten. It bogged down after ten, twenty, thirty pages— fifty seemed the magic number at which the most promising plots and characters refused to develop further.

I showed chapters of this ever-repeating project to Elena's boyfriend, a heart surgeon at Martin Luther King, Jr. Hospital who had a contract for a "Michael Crichton-type" medical thriller. (All of this later proved to be fictitious, including the heart surgeon part. He really was a doctor, though.) Bill was, or pretended to be, the nicer sort of Southern good ol' boy, as corpulent and watery-eyed as a gruff but kind-hearted Mississippi lawman, with a drawling, croaking baritone that made even dumb remarks sound richly considered and ironic. He did a fair deal of huffing, ruminating, and swabbing his glasses with his shirttails before allowing that I was "on the raaht traack." I wasn't, really, but I was grateful for any encouragement.

"See, what you have heah, is the beginnin' of a vary lihvley comin'-a-age bill-dungs romahn. I'm sortah shootin' for moah a best-sellin' suspense fiction narrative along the lines a Comah. You know what yuh really ought to whrite about is that . . . seamy homasesual world yoah livin' in."

I felt barely in the world at all, as the world of other people was fractured into drastically different quadrants: the punks I knew from the clubs, the middle-class lawyers and their families and friends I knew from work, and the gays in the pickup bars. I wasn't truly close to anybody, even Dane. I spent an absurd amount of time alone, in the car, driving nowhere in particular, driving because being on the road felt less horrifying than sitting alone in a room.

I often found myself driving on an unpaved access road that slithered along ridges hemmed with pines and juniper bushes to a flat, dusty plateau right below the observatory on Mount Lee. There was an outcrop of jagged travertine with caves woven through it. Sometimes I walked around in the caves, through puddles of bat guano, wary of rattlesnakes. Around a bend in the road, the reverse side of the Hollywood sign came into view, the letters, held up on charred diagonal pylons, a bricolage of white-painted metal sheets pocked with bullet holes. The ledge the sign perched on revealed a startling panorama, the city spread out below like an endless construction site sprinkled with talcum powder.

The sign had seen better days. Arsonists and kids with guns had attacked it. The scabby ground was strewn with used condoms and smashed beer bottles. The melancholy decrepitude suggested a moonscape in daylight, painted by Caspar David Friedrich in collaboration with Walt Disney. I dragged one of the scrunched, shot-off panels to my car and jammed it into my car trunk.

Installed in my bedroom at the Bryson, the battered metal resembled a John Chamberlain sculpture with a Cy Twombly painting scratched into its facing. The people who came to my apartment were not the type to have those references, and probably wondered if I was as geeky as this pointless acquisition seemed to indicate.

"Did you realize all those letters are actually full of holes?" I would ask them excitedly. "They look all solid white and shiny from a distance, but they're really not."

None of my guests found this intriguing, or my possession of something blown off a giant letter *O* with a shotgun remarkable. After a few weeks I didn't find it remarkable either, but getting rid of it would have been more trouble than keeping it around.

I continued writing my changeling novel, recording the flatline uneventfulness of my days, in an over-salted, mawkishly sad, alphabetic monotone, as if awaiting deliverance from purgatory. Periodically, I tore it up and started over from scratch. Since I had no idea how to publish anything and didn't believe the books I started were "real writing," this felt like a private struggle to understand why I had ended up on a hamster wheel of wage slavery and drunken sexual abandon. I often sensed that I'd gone beyond rescue and ruined the future, that my grasp of reality was probably even more defective than that of my parents, secure in their provincial New Hampshire microcosm.

I had the sense of always standing a little apart from the narrative, of missing the point, of nothing ever being quite enough or never adding up. Life was a choppy sequence of episodes and images unfolding in several worlds whose only connection was the fact that I slipped into one after another like an actor performing several plays in the same twenty-four-hour span.

The Bryson apartment filled up with books, stacks of books creeping up the walls, books on the china cabinet shelves, books piled on tables and stuffed in closets. I had hundreds more books than I could ever read, the majority shoplifted from Chatterton's, a bookstore on Vermont Avenue that had the performance space of a theater company in back.

I developed a crush on a married clerk at Chatterton's named Don, an actor in the theater company, whose rimless glasses, chipped front tooth, and wild hair made him look like a sexy space alien. In fact, he later played a space alien, in a series of moderately successful, low-budget science fiction films. I pursued him with the recklessness peculiar to the young and clueless. I wrote him love letters. I mooned around the store when he was working. He accepted these letters with a flirtatious amusement but never indicated any reciprocity of feeling. He liked the attention. The bookstore was the hub of a small band of literary types where nothing went unnoticed, and this low-burning erotic flame was soon noticed by everybody, and became another desultory gossip item. After I realized how public it all was, my infatuation became "ironic," a swooning joke: love is embarrassing. The adoring letters began to read like parodies of adoring letters, intended not only for his eyes but his wife's, his co-workers', even random customers. There was something ugly about all this, as if I were turning myself inside out and exposing my guts as a form of stand-up comedy.

At Chatterton's, too, I made friends with Mary Power, who worked the register on certain weekdays, and Vilma, her girlfriend, who managed the Los Feliz, a Laemmle theater, a few steps north on Vermont Avenue. Mary was a serious, soft-spoken, strong-chinned Irish woman with an uncanny gift of mimicry that she unleashed at dinner after many drinks. Vilma was short and pinch-faced, no beauty, but somehow a woman of laconic mystery, severe, occasionally volatile, defensively secretive. There were parties where most of the bookstore employees swanned around each other's apartments and backyard gardens, a pizza joint across Vermont where they gathered on Friday nights, a strip-mall bar on Hillhurst where everyone drank too much. Members of the Chatterton set were forever on the verge of starting or finishing a play, a novel, closing a screenplay deal, moving away to open a secondhand bookshop in Michigan, or to grow perfect weed in Humboldt County. On the face of it, however, nobody was in any hurry to do anything, even the clerks approaching middle age.

Mary encouraged me to continue stalking Don in my desultory fashion. She couldn't stand him. Behind my back, she berated him for leading me on and breaking my young heart. It sounds ridiculous now, but his sexual indifference embarrassed me for years after this whole period was finished, as a high point of humiliation. It was a purely willful, physical attraction, but I had fastened on Don as the person I wanted to love me back, imagining my desire could make this person I didn't really know into the person I wanted him to be. Unless I am greatly mistaken, the man himself was actually much less interesting than the space alien he one day incarnated, and, for that matter, less interesting than the man I was actually sleeping with. An unlimited obtusity governed my relationships with all sorts of people, particularly "romantic" manias that never found an appropriate object. Dane was easy, available for sex, and even, in his less-than-impressive way, devoted to me. Yet for that reason, I didn't place much importance on the real relationship we had, and invested my emotions in one that I didn't have.

Mary managed a Laemmle theater in Westwood at night, the Westland Twins, and offered me a moonlighting job selling tickets and running the concession stand. It was an indisputable reason to avoid working overtime at night in Watts—which, drugs or no drugs, had turned really scary with a slew of drive-by homicides a few blocks from the office—and promised to fill even more time with routine, away from the depressed solitude of my apartment. My writing wasn't really getting anywhere. I didn't think it

ever would. I supposed I would have to make some miserable compromise with reality in the near future. I'd go back to university and finish my degree, then become something unimportant and standardized in academia. Since I couldn't bear thinking about that, I figured the theater job, which ran till eleven p.m., would leave exactly enough free time to reach West Hollywood by midnight, have a few drinks, pick up a trick, get fucked, and fall asleep by three or four a.m. Except for drive time, there wouldn't be a single minute in there to think about anything.

Elena felt undermined by news of my second job, which would leave her completely alone after dark in a senseless-killing neighborhood. She became stingy with her surplus Eskatrol, which was supposed to reward me for staying in Watts after hours. I pleaded, begged, and promised to become a monster of office efficiency until she doled out a few precious capsules. The drug tended to soften her long-term memory, so if I waited a few days I could usually wheedle more from her. But this was too contingent on

Elena's mercurial moods, and I started looking for other sources. Skot, the nerdy-genius-looking ringleader of Science Holiday, put me on to a dealer named Benny, who, actually, sold bennies, as well as opies, dexies, and downers. The new supplier quickly became difficult. After I scored from him a few times at the House of Pies in Los Feliz, Benny decided that we would be friends.

"I like the way your mind works," he told me. These have always been ominous words, regardless of who says them. "We should hang out."

Hanging out with dealers is never much of an idea. Drop the wrong word, state a contrary opinion, reject their advances, or decline to read their poetry, and you can kiss your drug supply good-bye. You may also discover, as I did with Benny, that the mind of a dealer is quite twisted enough in a drug transaction without risking greater exposure to it.

Benny, who had suggestions of Ratso Rizzo in his general affect as well as his physiognomy—a great limp mane of oily black hair, and a reedy frame he covered in stained pinstripes and pointed ankle boots—had taken up permanent residence in the darkest side of nighttime Los Angeles, where people on copious drugs were unfixed in space and time, their movements determined by random phone calls at all hours from strung-out customers and far-gone freaks throwing parties. There were no cell phones in those days, dealers relied on answering services, pagers, and a network of public phones. I went to lots of parties with Benny, each weirder than the next, in pitch-dark apartments where clumps of wild-eyed protoplasm huddled around amplifiers or tables streaked with coke or powdered meth. An enormous amount of imperious staring went on at these soirees, where any social interaction only served as a time filler, instantly dropped the second more drugs arrived.

Benny's customers had a scary Manson Family smell wafting off them. They had other smells, equally unappealing. Everything moved too quickly, or else with slothlike slowness, from one sinister tribal meeting to another, each a tableau of spiked hair and scads of cloudy syringes, bleary interiors sealed in a bubble of amber silence, often dominated by some garrulous vampire with an unimaginable backstory and a cruel mouth. No inhibitions then about sharing needles, so people often had the waxy yellow pallor of hepatitis under their ghoulish makeup.

Some were livid faces I'd noticed in clubs, or glimpsed in coffee shop windows, and it sometimes gave me a little thrill to find out where the faces lived, what things they kept in their refrigerators, who their familiars were. One avid girl with zeppelin tits who dressed exclusively in spangled Lurex had a bungalow on lower Beachwood where possums and other wildlife meandered in and out of her living room through holes in the walls. A man who looked like Basil Rathbone as a child had turned his rambling flat into a papier-mâché cave, a womb where his associates nodded out for days on heroin, rousing themselves from hibernation with shots of meth, unpredictably flailing around like sped-up cartoon figures while still submerged in private dreams, shouting at invisible adversaries, uncertain whether they were in a loft downtown or somewhere in Century City or possibly in Echo Park or even West Adams.

In short, Benny lived among the lunatic undead. Far from having a consuming interest in the way my mind worked, he was vigilantly concerned about how my car

worked, since his ancient Camry had been kaput for weeks
and he had recently been moving around on buses. Public
transport carried a taint of pennilessness unhelpful in
Benny's profession, in which making people wait for
calculated periods of time was an essential skill. Like the
tenants of the Bryson, Bennie loved me for my car, and
not my golden hair.

He craved company, though. His face lit up when I
agreed to drive him around. He had customers all over the
city, but none seemed engaged with him in a personal way.
He provided a service; they took him for granted. He
admired his buyers overmuch, or pretended to. He took a
speed-breathless interest in anything they said, but their
interest in him was visibly limited. At numerous stops I
had an impression of being hurried on our way after Bennie
made his deliveries.

"Benny's kind of a nothing," Skot told me, with the
casual cruelty of his torpid crowd.

I never pieced Benny's story together, only heard this
and that, here and there. His mother had hanged herself
in the family garage a few years earlier. His father, a celebrity
gynecologist, lived somewhere in Sylmar with his third
wife and owned a getaway cottage in Tahoe. Benny had
taught eighth grade in a Catholic girl's school, lost his job
over some mild sexual impropriety, and had qualified for
psychiatric disability that paid him a miniscule check every
month. For a small-time dealer, he moved a lot of product.
But also he took a lot of product, and was forever scraping
bottom like everyone he knew. He was twenty-eight or -nine.
I imagined anyone slightly older, or slightly taller, as infinitely
worldlier and more sophisticated, less vulnerable, less
clueless—I never imagined him as immature and as scared
by living as I was, somehow it eluded me.

As most people running on amphetamine do, Benny talked too much, talked incessantly, seemed to be talking even when he wasn't talking, talked in his sleep no doubt, talked to walls if there was no one else around to talk to. I won't say he had theories, that would be taking things too far. He had themes, various themes, that touched on everything and nothing in the known and unknown worlds. He talked about Rimbaud and Beckett and William Burroughs, Heinrich von Kleist, Coomaraswamy, Buckminster Fuller, Norman O. Brown, cannibalism, Karl Marx. He talked about invisible things, telepathic transactions, imperceptible rumblings in the San Andreas fault, how he knew that person x would be at Licorice Pizza at such and such an hour, why he had an unquenchable lust for schoolgirls in uniform. Everything in his head spilled out of him in a torrent, excitedly, as if his brain were having an orgasm. He was one of the few people who have ever literally given me a headache.

Yet speed makes people oddly tolerant of anything happening around them, even when their heads are exploding. Although I perceived a definite need to detach myself from Benny's sphere in the middle future, this didn't come entirely into focus until one night when I drove him home, to a peculiarly situated one-story house that was little more than a shack on stilts, somewhere in Laurel Canyon, and let him talk me into coming in.

I have seen many chaotic interiors, as we all have, and lived in plenty of them too, but I only remember a few occasions when I walked into someone's living space and confronted a disorder so incomprehensible that it scared me out of my wits. Once, in New York, after J. J. Mitchell and I had snorted a terrifying quantity of poppers standing in the bar at Second Avenue and Fourth, we accepted an invitation from a man whose name I've forgotten—no, I haven't, it was Dicken, like the singular of Dickens—to continue drinking and snorting poppers in his apartment, a place in Turtle Bay where the entire floor surface proved to be covered in a thick mulch of trash. Not only was it carpeted in rich, loamy garbage, but this garbage was concealed under spread-out newspapers. Worse, in order to locate some little object he wanted, our host plunged his hand into the exact spot in this tremulous mess where whatever it was—a cigarette lighter? a cock ring?— happened to be located. In effect, he had a mental navigational map of the waste matter strewn over every inch of his apartment, and all his non-refuse items like keys and clothing and money were mixed in with things like takeout containers full of rotting spareribs, empty Orangina bottles, beer cans, pizza crusts, cigarette butts, and anything else likely to act as a magnet for vermin.

But Benny's hillside home easily eclipsed even that stupendous disarray. Stepping into his living room was like entering the scrambled brain of a serial killer through a portal of used motor oil. Garbage covered not only the floor but the chairs, tables, sofa, and every other available surface. And this was the tip of the iceberg, because much of the rear wall, perched over a graduated canyon slope, had been somehow demolished, as if a giant fist had punched through it. There was simply no physical boundary between the living room and the outdoors, and the slope itself was covered in even more garbage. It resembled a municipal dump. This dump had an oddly theatrical look, as if its contents had been carefully groomed for a visually arresting effect. It appeared that Benny had been tossing his detritus, organic and other, into this open area ever since moving into the house.

Of course, in tropical countries, open-sided houses or houses with open courtyards are unexceptionally common. Even in the jungles of Colombia and Peru, I have stayed in such houses, entirely open to the elements and dangerous predators, without the slightest alarm. However, Benny's house, on the distaff side of Los Angeles, seemed to be dissolving like fertilizer into its unsanitary yard, if I may call it that. His profusion of waste looked like a welcome wagon for coyotes and mountain lions.

The truly alarming thing was that Benny apparently lived in this rococo squalor as if it were the most unremarkable of human environments. I seldom listened closely to anything he said, but as he slogged through squishy heaps of grunge to the kitchen, came back with two cans of beer, handed me one, then cleared mountains of shit from a chair seat and a bit of the sofa, dug a glass bong from somewhere in the surrounding rubble, and proceeded to fill it with weed, I became aware that he was blathering incoherently about Friedrich Nietzsche, specifically something about superior beings destroyed by pity, and "the clever animals have to die." I also noticed that Benny's dark brown, sometimes black eyes had taken on a certain blazing, fanatical sheen. The Ratzo Rizzo aspect of his face had hardened into a hungry-looking rodent visage.

He inhaled a massive hit, then jumped up and bleated out through a thick nimbus of smoke:

"I know! You wanna see something really gross?"

Without waiting for an answer, Benny tramped off into another room. After an interlude of indefinable thrashing noises he returned, holding between his hands what appeared to be a small aquarium with a large clump of matter inside it, not floating, exactly, but suspended in clear, hardened glue. As he brought it closer, the clump became legible as . . . a dead cat. A partially flattened, dead little tabby with its eyes open, its mottled orange and white fur frozen forever in a state of shock.

"Oh my God."

I threw up a little. In that place it didn't matter.

"I didn't kill it! Some car ran over it on Franklin Avenue!"

"Okay, but still—"

"Yeah, but look at it, right? It's like art or something."

"I can't look, will you put that fucking thing away?"

"You wouldn't say that if you walked into a museum and saw this."

"I don't see that happening, Benny. But all right. It's . . . nice."

"No, it's gross. What did Picasso say? You do it first ugly, then other people do it pretty?"

"Right, it's nice and gross . . . please, I'm sensitive."

"It kind of changes colors in the light." Benny planted the aquarium down on a pile of magazines and stomped around the room to view it from different vantage points.

"It has a kind of chiaroscuro thing going on, there's these ripples that are like those scattery types of clouds."

"Uh-huh. Yeah, I can see that. Do you have anything more to drink?"

Who could know that in ten or fifteen years a larger version of Benny's aquarium with a different animal in it would be worth millions of dollars?

He's insane, I thought, taking an agitated hit off the bong. He's insane, and he's brought me here to kill me. For the fun of it, probably, like Leopold and Loeb. Then he'll have his own car to drive. My car. Little seedpods of sweat popped out all over my skin, paranoia amped up by grass. Yes, this rat-faced bastard was going to murder me and dump the body out on the trash heap.

Benny's face leaned into my face. His eyes bore into my eyes. His wolf-rat or rat-wolf expression laughed at my frightened-mouse expression. He droned on in his heavy voice, about something, something, puffing sententiously on an unfiltered Camel, and he looked absolutely ancient, as if thirty or forty years of the future had abruptly piled up on his face.

My trepidation subsided into an altogether different perception of Benny's acute loneliness and social ineptitude. At his friends' houses he fawned over certain individuals who made him nervous, excessively flattered people he felt afraid of . . . his consistent failure to charm, and now, here, in his own lair, all this ominous, ingratiating blabber about Nietzsche . . . and the dead cat . . . the thought arrived, finally: nobody really likes their drug dealer.

"I haven't slept in like, four days." Benny brought this out with the haggard, chain-dragging weariness of the Ghost of Christmas Past.

"Have you been eating?" I asked, feeling cornered into assuming a maternal concern that didn't suit me at all.

"Yeah, I had some tacos at that stand on Hillhurst," he said with considerable pathos.

"When was that?"

"Yesterday, I think. Yes, definitely yesterday."

"Benny, you can't keep taking this shit and not eat," I said, sounding more and more like my mother. I hadn't completely shaken the idea of him as a homicidal maniac, and remembered reading somewhere that if you thought someone might kill you, you should try to make them see you as a human being like themselves. "I force myself. I tell myself, 'Gary, your body is all you have.' Otherwise when you come down it's a train wreck. Look, I'll drive you to Tommy's. Eat a burrito. It's right by where I live. You can stay there tonight if you feel like it."

The thought of Benny sleeping at my place horrified me. But if I didn't get out of there soon, I would end up sleeping at his place, an even more horrible prospect.

"Eating, shitting, fucking, sleeping. That's about all there is, isn't it. No wonder people go berserk."

"Is that a yes or a no? At least take a Tuinal and get some rest."

Benny pulled off his boots and sprawled himself across the couch, as if to say that rubbish was his home and he would never spurn it for faraway places.

"Tuinal . . . is . . . such . . . a . . . pansy . . . drug. No offense or anything."

After drinking six or seven beers and smoking two packs of cigarettes on meth autopilot, I felt ready to vomit again. Benny seemed less and less menacing. Riding the wiggy oscillations of an onrushing speed crash, he'd grown lachrymose and expansive, even abject, and came close to sobbing as he went mournfully on about what a great scene had been there in LA in the old days, by which I felt certain he meant only a few days earlier.

"Everything was new. You could reach out your hand and touch it, it was all there." His hand reached into the queasy emptiness of the universe in quest of this nebulous everything, displaying grimy nails. "It was really only a few people, everyone knew you, you knew everyone . . . I never thought things could change like that," he concluded, snapping his fingers.

"I'm not clear what you're telling me," I said, unsure what to do with my face. I felt a pressing need to escape Benny's highly emotional aura before it crystallized into something depressingly stark and terrible. There is nothing

comforting in one addict telling another to look forward
to a brighter day, so I refrained from extolling the virtues
of food any further. "Anyway, I have to get up and go to
work in the morning."

I couldn't stop answering his calls: answering machines
were an expensive novelty, the concept of "screening" didn't
exist. So I kept one excuse or another not to see him on file
in my head, ready on the first ring, and deflected him long
enough that he stopped phoning me. I couldn't separate
Benny from the image of his psychotic environment, the
dead cat, and the spectacular morbidity and self-loathing
they portended. This left a significant gap in the drug
stockpile, until Dane tented a house in Calabasas owned
by a croaker who wrote him a script for Obitrol.

It often happens that an expected storm fails to materialize, or proves less spectacular than anticipated. Hours and hours of media airtime are cleared to cover it. Television reporters are deployed to ocean-side locations where large waves are churning in the background, and close-ups of puddles are said to represent "the eye of the storm." The expectation of catastrophe becomes impatience at its not arriving, with the threat of boredom becoming palpable desperation to fill "dead air."

twelve

This afternoon I took a cab to the Plaza de Armas, thinking
I might buy a watch for J. I'd prefer to buy him a crumbly,
century-old photo album. But those albums are enormous
and weigh tons. Impossible to ship, because it's Cuba and
the gift would arrive a year from now, if ever. Impossibly
heavy in my luggage. Anyway, an immigration officer might
figure out I've been here from looking at the album. (The
intelligence services know anyway but aren't supposed to.)
It's illegal in a convoluted way. It's legal to physically travel
here, but illegal to spend any money, because the embargo
falls under the authority of the Treasury Department.

   I already went through the Joe McCarthy rigmarole you
have to endure if you're caught, a few years ago. I nipped
that third degree in the bud after twenty minutes, in a
detention facility at the Lester B. Pearson International
Airport in Toronto. After the third body search and the
fourth forensic study of every item in my luggage, I forced
through my teeth the news that I was dying from untreatable
cancer, and had gone to visit lifelong friends, "probably
for the last time." "I'm an old man, and I'm going be dead
soon," I said, working up to showstopping, histrionic,
artfully class-inflected anger and bitterness. *"Do you mind?"*
As I said this I broke into copious sobs, choked back tears
to blow my nose in a Kleenex, apologized for being so

emotional, and burst into tears again. Finally the horrified
tub of lard from immigration, his voice suddenly benign
and laced with cancer terror, said, "I think we're done
here." I wasn't an actor in my salad days for nothing.

I've never worn a watch in my life. I felt an unfamiliar
need today to know what time it is. The watches were all
overpriced, mostly broken.

I drank a coffee at a place on O'Reilly Street. They used
to serve simple fried chicken there, with crispy skin. That's
been substituted by a chicken cutlet seared in a grid of
unappetizing cubes. It tasted like pencil shavings. Chicken
is the only thing you get to eat in Cuba, chicken and pork.
In Pinar del Río or Las Tunas you might get a piece of
fish. People in other places never believe how gross the
food is when I tell them. They have a fantasy of food in the
Caribbean tropics inspired by Carmen Miranda's headgear.
If you find a single spot in Havana serving a single dish
half as good as the same thing served in Ecuador, chances
are you will eat there daily instead of risking what you
might find on your plate in the place next door.

In my opinion, so-called Caribbean cuisine is vile on
all the islands, but Cuba is the standout of *mare nostrum.*
(I suppose people who go to St. Barts fly their food in from
France, but anyone who'd want to be on the same island
with those people has to be insane.) Cuban food is so
memorably hideous that you can tell if some bullshit person
has ever actually been here by getting them to talk about
the food.

A few nights ago, an Argentine friend, contemplating
the squalid profusion of hustlers gathered along the Malecón,
came up with an enticing tourist pitch: "You'll come for
the prostitutes, but you'll stay for the food." I was counting
on this restaurant's chicken, and it betrayed me.

I reconsidered buying a gift watch. Maybe a pricey, pre–Revolution Cuba pocket watch. That way I could tell time here, and have a present to give later. The watches rested on squares of navy felt beside an array of Camilo Cienfuegos lapel pins and novelty items from the 1940s.

The man selling watches pesters me. He thinks he's a mind reader. These vendors would sell more if they left the customers alone instead of trying to guess what they're looking for. How would I know what I'm looking for until I find something I want in this flea market mess? But the sellers here love to put me in a stranglehold of boredom. They try for sweet, but come off overbearing and tiresome. Plus their pushiness—in Istanbul at the Grand Bazaar, merchants are in your face too, but on them it's mercenary exuberance; here it looks pathetically like desperation. They've trained themselves on tourists, who are stupid by nature and fascinated by any shiny object waved in front

188 I CAN GIVE YOU ANYTHING BUT LOVE

of them. So the vendors presume stupidity in everyone, and have lost any radar for the non-stupid. On top of that, most of them are quite stupid themselves.

A tiny Coca-Cola crate, its little grid filled with teeny milky-green bottles. Beside that, sad bracelet charms, a Bakelite binocular viewer, and a box of slides that don't fit into the viewer. Held up to the sun they reveal views of Egyptian pyramids and other Wonders of the World, in soft rotogravure colors: Angel Falls, Great Wall of China, Porcelain Tower of Nanjing.

Puckered *National Geographics* from the 1930s. Copies of *Life* with scarred covers of Cardinal Mindszenty, quintuplets, Amelia Earhart, General Eisenhower. On another table, betting chips in a plastic slide caddy: a few from old Mafia casinos in Havana, others from Deauville and Las Vegas. On two chips, a swastika incised at the center winks luridly, like the bad uncle who suddenly sticks his hands down your pants.

The chip owner surveys his wares with the shrewd boredom of a diamond dealer whose merchandise will always find a buyer and never take a stock dive, sitting spread out like a sack of sawdust in a canvas chair, smoking a Cohiba cigar. He's aloof. Can't be bothered. Customers try his patience. When he thinks of it he scratches the ear of a mangy, pregnant dog. It looks like he's recently eaten something preferable to chicken.

"¿Cuanto es?"

"Those? Those are very expensive."

They are. Sixty CUCs per chip. Slightly less than seventy dollars. I guess it's worth it, but I haven't got it. I do, really, but it's too frivolous to pay seventy dollars for one poker chip. Even one with a swastika on it. Funny that Nazi memorabilia is as prized in the worker's paradise as anywhere else.

Céline missed this detail in his *fin-de-guerre* trilogy: casino chips of the Third Reich. How did they get here? But wait, what am I thinking? He describes the casino in the Hotel Simplon in Baden-Baden in *North*, July 1944, the same passage I read in John Boskovich's film twelve or thirteen years ago: *"the dexterity of luck! . . . harmonious unbroken movements, chips . . . flawless delivery! . . . the tradition of the Baden Casino doesn't date from yesterday! . . . Berlioz played there and Liszt . . . and all the Romanov princes . . . the Naritzkins and Savoys . . . the Bourbons and Braganças . . ."* I walk into the park behind the lined-up felt tables and propped-open display cases and fish out my notebook, and start outlining an "adventures of a penny" story, describing the travels of a Nazi poker chip from a punter's breast pocket in Baden-Baden in 1944 to a roulette table at Meyer Lansky's Riviera in the last days of Batista. But the pencil starts to drag me back to California, having a lazy will of its own.

That was years after anyone holding that poker chip would have cashed out on a permanent basis. I wonder what's underneath what I recall. Secrets? Wishes? Longings? Wishes, longings: so simpler to remember than whatever I thought I was doing.

I must have told myself comforting things to account for the fear and inertia I experienced interchangeably. Fear of being nothing, of being damaged beyond repair, fear of being remembered only by people I wanted to forget. In the car. On the freeway. In a bar. Wasting eons of irrecoverable time.

I must have pretended life was a novel or a movie I was narrating as it went along, as if I had control of it and decided what direction it took. I see now that at the time

I've been writing about, there was no coherent point to me at all.

Leaving the park this afternoon I suddenly felt sick of Havana. I stayed in a black mood until the sun went and night settled over everything. Sick of clouds and the sky and the sea and the rest of it. I came back to the apartment. I tried to read a Spanish edition of *Othello* I bought in the Plaza de Armas. I went out again to feed the cats.

★

The Westland Twins provided a limited but exciting view of Hollywood glamour and money. We showcased a specific grade of "foreign" movie: European, with subtitles, a notch or two below the artistic level of Fassbinder, Buñuel, Godard, or Pasolini. Probably the only first-class films we ran were edgy melodramas by Claude Chabrol. The better movies played at the Los Feliz in Los Feliz, the Pico in West Hollywood, and the Nuart in Santa Monica. Our offerings were undemandingly arty, slightly pretentious, domestic farces or dramas of middle-class marriage gone awry, or Italian sex comedies of the frou-frou type that featured the Antonioni-less Monica Vitti.

A typical night began with Mary stocking the cash drawer and organizing receipts from the matinee shift. A buxom, giddy queen named Kevin and I filled the fake butter dispenser and then replenished the soda spigots. The cloying odors of stale candy and artificial butter were nauseating, but somehow stimulating too. In its own absurd way, working in a movie house wasn't entirely unlike being in a movie or on stage as an extra.

Mary was forever on the phone with Max Laemmle, scion of the Laemmle empire, nephew of Carl Laemmle,

founder of Universal Studios. Carl Laemmle's latter days as CEO had been marked by his habit of attending board meetings carrying a piss bucket, owing to a failing bladder. Max himself was now completely gaga. He spent his days placing frantic calls to his various theaters in a state of dementia. On one occasion he demanded to know where Vilma was.

"She's right there in the office, with you," Mary told him.

"This woman with black hair?"

"Yes, that's Vilma."

"Then where is Mary?"

"I'm Mary."

"Well, Mary, I'm hanging up, if you hear from Vilma tell her to call me."

"Max is such a character," Mary always said when she got off the phone.

A bit later, Sam, our projectionist, sauntered in through the service door and grabbed a few snacks from the shelves, then disappeared into his booth. Sam, a blandly good-looking, tall, gangly Texan, was the object of Kevin's predatory lust. At the theater, Kevin killed a lot of downtime by scheming to get Sam loaded after work.

"I don't care if he pretends afterward it never happened, I'm gonna rim that delicious asshole if it's the last thing I do."

Whenever Sam came out of the booth to use the rest room, Kevin immediately had to pee. "His cock is the size of a donkey's," he reported on several occasions. "Really. It's as big as the Ritz. Like Porfirio Rubirosa!"

Having studied Sam closely myself, I thought this was probably true.

"And he wants it," Kevin added. That sounded less plausible. I could often recognize my pathology in other people while remaining blind to my own.

The theater drew audiences from Bel Air, Brentwood, and other fabulously rich neighborhoods. Westwood was an easy drive for them. "The rustle of money" is no idle phrase. Our customers, any one of whom had more money than twenty blocks of Watts would cost, were somehow effortlessly misted in wealth. It exuded from their pores. Their clothes looked ineffably finer, more vivid, better fitted, somehow cleaner than ordinary people's clothes. Their hairstyles looked engraved, hair by individual hair, into archetypal hairstyles worthy of museum mannequins. They wore the subtlest jewelry, string-thin platinum bracelets, teardrop opal earrings, demure-looking diamond rings, and you knew the stones were worth as much as the building they were standing in.

This never stopped the clientele from complaining about the price of Twizzlers or a cup of Sprite, which hardly cost anything.

"A bag of M&Ms never *used* to be seventy-five cents," some face-lifted hag in a ranch mink would opine, in an access of longing for an earlier, more gracious era when M&Ms had cost fifty cents.

Notable figures graced our lobby. Anjelica Huston. Tony Perkins. I sometimes asked for their autographs on dispenser napkins, then took somewhat childish pleasure in using the napkins to mop up Coke spills. The only customer who ever acted like a prick about giving an autograph wasn't even a big star—Graham Jarvis, who had played Charlie Haggers on *Mary Hartman, Mary Hartman*, seemed to view being recognized as a criminal importunity.

I was barely noticed by the customers. I may have been cute enough to be considered fuckable earlier in the day, but I arrived at the theater wilted-looking from my Watts job, and in any case, people don't really register anybody selling them popcorn in a movie theater. Two customers who did go out of their way to be personable were Robert Wagner and Natalie Wood. They acted like teenagers in love, always made friendly conversation, and were generous with tips. (No reputable business, in those days, featured a tip jar. "RJ" would, however, slide a dollar bill across the counter, and wink.)

Three nights a week, the freeway system became an umbilicus between the shittiest ghetto in America and the country's richest suburb. The surreal contrast between the two places formed my entire world view, which hasn't altered much since.

Stefan—please come to hotel at 6-6:30 Alabin 67 off Vitosha Blvd please do not fuck anybody else this afternoon I want you to write yr name in cum on my face w yr cock (not yr patronymic just yr first name)
Sent from iPhone, Sofia, Bulgaria, August 2013

thirteen

The ghost of Ernest Hemingway would like to haunt the isle of Cuba. In Miramar there is the Hemingway Marina. Several bars and hotels in Habana Vieja display portraits of Hemingway in various heroic poses on their walls. A famous Hemingway daiquiri is served in many places. The flea market stalls in the Parque Cespedes have sold disintegrating paperbacks of *Adiós a las Armas* and *El Viejo y el Mar*, and sometimes books by Hemingway in English, in all the years I have come here.

Most Cubans have never read Hemingway and never will. In fact most Cubans have no idea who Hemingway was, and only recognize the name as that of the marina, or, in some cases, the famous daiquiri. The myth of Ernest Hemingway as a Cuban national idol has not enjoyed much traction since the 1960s, when Hemingway and Fidel Castro were often photographed together, smoking cigars or sharing a comradely embrace.

Now that Norman Mailer has joined the shades of ancient evenings, the only American writer who still carries a torch for Ernest Hemingway is Joan Didion, upon whom the influence of Hemingway has not been entirely wonderful. The irksome repetitions and overly precious one-line paragraphs in Didion come directly out of Hemingway and the pregnant white space he famously left around his sentences. The tough, laconic, manly men who serve as fantasy heroes in Didion's fiction have the unmistakable Hemingway touch. So do the shrieking pansies and suicidal homos she scatters through her books for spice, like pineapple rings on a Christmas ham. If Didion did not have the mind of a steel trap up her sleeve, she would be Ernest Hemingway, much to the detriment of American letters.

Hemingway and Marilyn Monroe are often thought of in the same breath, so to speak. They reached their zenith of celebrity and committed suicide around the same time. They embodied certain fantasies and gender stereotypes rampant in the 1950s. Yet we still love Marilyn, whose genius on the screen is there to see, and her sad private story continues to move us, even when recounted by a twaddle factory in Princeton, New Jersey. Hemingway we love considerably less. His genius on the page seems ever more indiscernible, as he moves ever closer to the realm of antiquary curiosity where Fannie Hurst and thousands of Hula-Hoops have gathered dust for half a century.

How did it happen? Why, why, why did the creator of Lady Brett Ashley and Jake with the missing testicle sink so precipitously in our regard? Hemingway is a lousy writer. A phony writer. A writer whose books are a tissue of falsehoods and moronic clichés of masculinity. A mendacious, ridiculous, deluded buffoon of a writer intoxicated by fame to the point of writing drivel. A malicious, unscrupulous, pig-headed bully who stole any good idea he ever had from his betters and turned those ideas into banalities. A Harlequin romance novelist masquerading as a pioneer of literary modernism.

But none of that has ever tarnished the esteem enjoyed by other male, heterosexual, American writers of

Hemingway's vintage or Hemingway's sensibility in such a dramatic way. F. Scott Fitzgerald may not have been as big a prick as Hemingway (literally, if Hemingway himself can be believed, and he can't), but his books are even worse than Hemingway's, including *The Great Gatsby*, which is often mistaken for a great novel because it can be read in a few hours and its characters are rich people who come to a bad end. Even Charles Bukowski hasn't yet diminished in his influence, and his books are—there is no polite way of saying it—shit. As for today's standard-bearers of normal love and the arduous quest involved in becoming a man, they are but pale suburban worms beside the behemoth of snowy Kilimanjaro.

Perhaps it's because time has peeled away the testosterone facial mask of this endlessly posturing, preening, pathetic cheerleader of the bullring and killer of elephants and tigers, revealing a callow sissy whom his transgendered son didn't hesitate to address as "her." Perhaps it's because white space so readily suggests an absence of mental activity instead of a plenum of immanent meaning. Perhaps it's simply the fact that daiquiris have gone out of fashion.

But before we dump his collected writings into the marina with which he is so often confused, bidding good riddance to once-sacred rubbish, and forget about Hemingway altogether, let's remember that Hemingway left a sizeable chunk of his fortune to his many cats and their successive offspring, who still enjoy a life of feline luxury in Florida. So Papa wasn't all bad after all.

★

NO, a punk zine, sent me to interview David Lynch, who had debuted his now-classic film *Eraserhead* at Filmex. We met at Tiny Naylor's on Sunset. Expecting a brain-fried freak with pitted skin and rotten teeth after watching the ingeniously gross *Eraserhead*, I prepared for this meeting by bleaching my hair white and spraying it orange, piercing my left nostril with a safety pin, and dressing like an escapee from a locked ward.

David Lynch turned out to be freaky in a completely different way than I anticipated. Nattily blazered and coiffed, his baby-smooth face as peppy and bland as a Rotary Club, he bore a striking resemblance to Mr. Potatohead. His large teeth gleamed. His hair, the color of wet straw, was worked into the high-crested '50s do favored by Troy Donahue or the now-forgotten Fabian Forte.

He talked about *Eraserhead* and himself with extreme single-mindedness. Without being asked, he declared that he had never ingested a drug or smoked a cigarette, and eschewed all stimulants, including coffee. He ordered a repulsive herbal beverage called Postum and stared reprovingly at my coffee cup as if it contained cyanide.

I had been fascinated by his hilarious film. But his enthusiasm about it was not infectious. He seemed spellbound by his own accomplishment, and had already decided what he was going to say about it. He had, he told me, formerly lived in Philadelphia. Living in Philadelphia had instilled in him such fear and dread that he might have been speaking of Auschwitz. He never explained why Philadelphia had so traumatized him. He seemed to imply that he'd lived in some grueling, impoverished, decrepit industrial hell like the setting of *Eraserhead*. This seemed doubtful to me: David Lynch had the inbred assurance of an upper-middle-class Eagle Scout, a wide-eyed, impervious optimism that only needed a dusting of freckles and a few amphetamines to turn him into Judy Garland in *The Wizard of Oz*.

He then described—for an hour—one particular, technically challenging zoom-in shot on something he referred to as a "crack o' wheat," apparently some ball-like, stationary object he'd placed at the end of a camera track, as if I would naturally know what a "crack o' wheat" was. I still have no idea. I still don't care, either.

The other consuming theme of our interview, to which he returned again and again in case I had overlooked its importance the first time, was the fact that Jack Nance, the film's lead actor, had had to wear the same bizarre Afro for five years because Lynch's production money had repeatedly dried up.

I disliked David Lynch immensely. His stories were humorless and boring. His smarmy air as he stirred his Postum was even creepier than his movie. However, it occurred to me that his tedious wholesomeness, so exaggerated that it seemed perverse in a way quite opposite to his movie, might be a brilliant ruse, like Magritte's formal dinner jackets.

"I would never agree to do a Hollywood-type film," he assured me, "unless I could make all the actors unrecognizably ugly."

He followed *Eraserhead* with *The Elephant Man*, a treacly tale with a message of tolerance for those who are different, in which Anne Bancroft, John Gielgud, Wendy Hiller, and Anthony Hopkins looked exactly the way they did in everything else, the only ugly standout being John Hurt as the eponymous Elephant Man.

People aren't expected to be happy, as an ongoing condition, anywhere on earth, not really, except in propaganda, advertising, sitcoms. Life is pessimistic because we die. How could it be otherwise? But when people spill into the abyss, they discover that they aren't allowed to be extremely unhappy as a chronic thing, either, and become the object of impatience, dread, fear—fear that their hopelessness is contagious, as in the case of the bus driver who ran over the soccer star.

fourteen

Melancholia is playing at the Milan cinema on La Rampa. I considered recommending it to P., having thought about this film for months, but she is the debutante type so common in the art world, familiar with proper names and the prices of various objects but completely uninterested in anything more demanding than a thumbnail reproduction and a press release. That's as true of many high-end dealers as it is of fringe figures like P., who caters receptions in her house, and arranges this and that for visiting artists. They all have the mentality of pork butchers who keep both thumbs on the scale. It's doubtful she would ever go to a movie house on La Rampa, anyway. Alcoholics and psychiatrists, I read somewhere, both avoid going to the movies.

Something was off with the projection, or the print, or both, it looked as if the movie I saw in New York had been run through a bath of Clorox, but it was still very powerful. I felt curious to see how a Cuban audience would react. People leaving the theater looked stunned. That might have been the Clorox effect. But they all dispersed quickly. I had no chance to eavesdrop on their conversations. When I first saw *Melancholia*, I was crawling out of my own living death, and the film pulled me right back into it. At the same time, the fact that someone had pictured this state of depressive alienation was, on some level, soothing. It confirmed something true about the melancholiac's view of the world, his/her indifference to its empty rituals and false emotions. Certainly by the time Justine tells Claire that "life on Earth is evil," the film has proven it in spades. "What kind of God," my father used to ask, "would have invented the food chain?"

I wondered if Lars von Trier experienced any benefit from the large number of people concerned about him, and decided probably not. When you go behind the moon, no one can follow you there to bring you back, and the quality of darkness is so overwhelming it can't be described. The words that could describe it, like most words, have been rendered meaningless by the hyperbole of vernacular speech. When everything is awesome and amazing, anything really out of the ordinary is practically inexpressible.

I also wondered if he deliberately piled on the operatic melancholia of Tristan and Isolde and Caspar David Friedrich in hopes that pushing it all beyond the pale would humor him back into a tolerable frame of mind. One is desperate for something to laugh about, even if it's the end of all existence in the universe. It is usual for people in depression to try anything, anything at all, to make it go away. But people in depression are also, usually, incapable of taking the smallest steps. Justine can't lift her foot to get into the bathtub. Meat loaf, the one thing she might be counted on to enjoy eating, tastes like ashes in her mouth, and she can't swallow it.

★

After Ferd reappeared, my sporadic contacts with Carol increased. Over the years she had called me from time to time, in a rush of maniacal inspiration to involve me in projects that had occurred to her on a jumbo dose of lithium, projects that became, sometimes for a few days, but usually for a few hours at most, all-consuming obsessions. Carol caught me in moments of drastic susceptibility, when my daily situation felt utterly shitty and hopeless, at the onset of clinical depression (mine). Although I knew her to be a seriously destructive person, who drew people into her narrative for the express purpose of turning on them and making them miserable, and used her biopolar disorder as an obnoxious weapon, she had a strangely powerful, arachnid glamour that made me feel closer to her than I did to many people I liked a lot better.

Her visits to LA were jarring, difficult longueurs. She had listened to the tapes I improvised driving to work—the cab driver, the terrorist, the studio hairdresser—and she sketched out a video project in which I would incarnate the characters. She sounded scarily but seductively enthusiastic, suggesting we commence as quickly as possible.

By the weekend, (her) depression had become so crippling that even lifting the phone to say she wasn't coming was an act too fraught with sensations of failure and guilt for her to go through with it. A few days later, her excitement became boundless again, a new date was set, but as it approached, her mind shifted again to the dark side, an abyss in which a simple phone call asking if her plans had changed was perceived as an act of savage aggression on my part.

The element of attrition involved in sustained interaction with Carol suggested the wisdom of keeping her at tongs' length. She actually came to the Bryson, finally, several times, lugging her Film Studies Sony Portapak, but each time was overwhelmed by ambivalence about whether it was the "right time" to shoot anything, considering the horrible mood she was in after driving all the way to LA from Goleta. When I suggested we might forget the whole thing for a while, that the world wouldn't crumble if the comedy gold of a few amphetamine ravings went untaped for posterity, Carol shrieked that I had "dragged" her into making these videotapes, forced her to make the crucifying drive to Los Angeles, and was now adding to her martyrdom by calling it all off. She was insane, as I've already mentioned.

All the same, the idea of a reunion of the three of us naturally suggested itself and then became an inevitability. I can only suppose we were all ridiculously driven to force our lives into a legible story line. Getting together would fill a worrisome blank space between 1969 and 1976. Carol and Ferd hated each other, but neither could admit it— that was too unsophisticated. During their Evanston period, Ferd had dutifully finished his MA at Northwestern, and Carol, I think, earned a PhD at the University of Chicago. They'd lived together in some dingy basement flat, in a hell of seething animosity. Arthur Ginsberg included scenes of their Evanston inferno as an epilogue to *The Adventures of Carol and Ferd*: they were grim, like Warhol's *Kitchen*, and the crapulous quality of half-inch black-and-white videotape made the two combatants appear submerged in an ocean of colorless cooking oil. Yet having divorced and lost track of each other, now that they knew each other's location, they were determined to prove they were adults, and had outgrown the murderous loathing they still felt for each other.

We went to a Directors Guild screening of Paul Schrader's *Blue Collar*. Afterward we went to my apartment for drinks. In the Bryson elevator, as he pulled the metal gate shut, Ferd sighed, with an oracular exhaustion I can still hear after thirty-five years: "There aren't going to be any more highs."

In that remarkable moment, a switch was thrown in my brain. I suddenly knew that I had expected, for years, the bleak atmosphere of the 1970s to blow away one sunny day like fog, and the good good times of the 1960s to roll back in. The sour, disillusioned era of Patty Hearst and Watergate and Baader-Meinhof, I realized, was not an interruption of the revolution—however I'd pictured *that*, if I'd pictured it at all—but an ugly portent of inevitable things to come, the first gasp of the final strangulation of human dreams. Reality would always be *harsh* reality, and the world would forever divide into winners and losers, and if you were wired the way we were, you would unavoidably end up a loser. Deluded as Ferd often was, I recognized that he'd said something true.

Some further outings ensued, but the novelty quickly wore off. An entrenched habit of instant contradiction, of sniping, sulfurous innuendoes suggestive of Tracy and Hepburn with Dexedrine hangovers, or two chittering rattlesnakes in a lethal mating dance, made their company unbearable. I felt implicated in their bilious outpourings, even responsible for their ugly feelings. The Carol and Ferd show dragged me to early evening cocktail lounges, some dinners at the then-only Japanese restaurant outside Japan Town, on Hoover. I felt like glue sticking them together when they should have inhabited different solar systems.

One night they descended in tandem on the Westland Twins, supposedly to watch a remake of *The Woman in the Window*, but really to watch me drudging behind the concession counter. I felt as if my own insignificance in their rejuvenated drama was their only point of friendly agreement, and that they'd come to the theater to deflect their mutual contempt by spilling it on me.

"Don't believe a word that person tells you," I told Mary after they'd gone into the auditorium.

"I thought she was an old friend of yours."

"Not by choice, I assure you."

But it is a choice, of course, a bad one that plays itself out over the remaining year in Los Angeles: Carol calls, in a dire, wheedling voice implores me to drive up to where she lives in Goleta one Saturday when the rains are so violent the radio warns of possible mud slides on the PCH. When I arrive at her motel-like apartment complex, she refuses to let me in, as if she never made the call and I have rudely invaded her privacy. She orders her boyfriend, a spineless teahead with shoulder-length hair, twenty years her junior, to shove a gift package into my hands in the doorway. All the way back down the coast, the car skids and slides over lakes of pounding rain, the wipers useless, the sheets of iron mesh holding various canyon walls in check threatening to burst at any moment, sending an avalanche of shit down the hills to fling the car into the Pacific.

I pull into Dart Square as the typhoon tapers down to a heavy drizzle, in front of the Rexall's where Aldous Huxley first dropped mescaline. I tear off the ridiculously festive wrapping paper and rip open the box to find an ashtray commemorating the Queen's Silver Jubilee, an Indian beaded belt, and a paperback collection of William Carlos Williams poems: what on earth does it mean?

Meanwhile, Ferd inquires, with urgent secrecy, if I'm willing to "store" something in my apartment. Something "we," meaning he and his commune, need to "keep somewhere else."

"It depends what it is, I'm not living in Versailles, you know."

"It's nothing big, it's the size of an Army foot locker, something like that. Like a steamer trunk. It would probably fit under your bed."

"You mean to say you don't have enough space for a trunk? I thought you guys had a house."

"It isn't that we don't have room . . . see, it's full of papers and stuff that—if we get raided, it's material that, you know, could be considered incriminating."

"What material? Diagrams of a hydrogen bomb?"

"Just underground papers, reports, minutes of meetings, but you know yourself, if they want to bust you for something and make a case—"

"Look, Ferd, if it would incriminate you, it would obviously incriminate me."

"No, it wouldn't."

"Oh, let's hear that old Cartesian reasoning, I dare you."

"For the simple reason that you're not doing anything suspicious. You're not under surveillance."

"And you are? Are you sure you're not paranoid?"

"Maybe, maybe not," he says with a shrug.

"If I agree," I tell him, "and you aren't paranoid, how do I know I won't end up like Kirilov in *Demons*?"

"I promise you won't," Ferd says. "Really, you *won't*." Then adds, Jesuitically, raising one drooping eyelid, "But isn't it exciting to think you might?"

The mysterious chest, a pigskin affair with metal corners, with a cheap padlock in front, was duly delivered, by Ferd and a tall bearded guy in overalls. We jammed it into a closet. I believe it was full of weapons, but I never opened it. I knew I was taking a stupid risk. I knew that most normal people would report a plot to blow up a building. I wasn't wired that way. I wasn't in the habit of calling the police about anything. I preferred to think nothing would happen. I was also curious to see if something would. Like many people at that time, I had no strong moral objections to the idea of terrorism, however messy its actual practice was.

A month later, two strangers from the commune showed up to recover the chest. This cryptic object and its secretive shuttle through the city seemed a logical part of the narrative, however indecipherable. The International Women's Conference came and went without explosion.

I sensed that things were advancing, despite the static atmosphere of that summer. Some missing pieces of the picture would click into place, the answers to barely formulated questions would rain from the skies. I could feel it the way you feel weather in your bones after a fracture.

Before the trunk removal, Dane was touchingly exercised

about its presence in my apartment.

"You don't even know the fuck's in it," he said. "What if it's a bomb and it goes off and kills you? I'll help you throw it out if you want."

It showed that he loved me a little, enough to feel protective, which counted for something. Since Dane was elusive and seldom around, and went through the world with the bright confidence and self-absorption of men hung like horses, I felt lucky when he surprised me with proprietary affection, although the affair was basically over. It had been agreed from the jump that it wouldn't be a long-term thing, that we would never constitute a "couple." But he had become something like a friend. He was leaving Los Angeles, either for Austin, where he had friends, or Miami, where they had bugs. He was anxious, he said, not to get "locked in" to one city, and if he could someday manage it, thought he might even move to Amsterdam, where you could buy hashish in a café and live on a houseboat. There was no shortage of household vermin wherever you went.

The thought of Dane leaving town was more distressing than the idea of never sleeping with him again. I had a horror of being left behind, of remaining stuck in a prison of habit while friends made bold changes in their lives. It seemed many people I knew were laying plans, plotting out futures, preparing to stake some claim to real existence in the ebb and flow of things, while I floundered like a formless blob, failing to acquire any consistent identity. I lacked the imagination or the will to abandon everything and fly to Amsterdam or Istanbul and figure out how to survive after getting there, which might have defined me in a more legible way, at the least as "an expatriate." I had published a few things, in some obscure places, but couldn't really call myself "a writer."

I hadn't accomplished a single thing. I continued my daily shuttle from Watts to Westwood, continued mooning over Don at Chatterton's, hitting the Masque on weekends, weekdays racing to the Detour and the One Way and the Spike to strike expressive poses in the two hours before closing, pick up strangers, fuck between two o'clock and four, and wake after three hours' sleep to jump on the hamster wheel all over again. Pasolini's *Salò* ran as a midnight movie at the Pico that season. As I knew the manager, I watched it about twenty times on a comp. *Salò* confirmed my view of the big picture: a world of slaves forced to eat shit by large, unattractive men.

My sole achievement at the time was a stapled, four-page xeroxed zine called *Teeny Duchamp Arrested for Shoplifting*, which I put together at the office and handed out at the cavernous Elks Hall during the now-legendary benefit for the Masque, which was losing its lease on the basement club off Hollywood Boulevard. It was a strange evening, in what was basically a retirement home reminiscent of Gloria Swanson's mansion in *Sunset Boulevard*, that started with a set by The Go-Go's and ended with a mini police riot that dispersed not only the benefit, but the seething nihilist energy that had been driving the punk scene. Actually, the scene continued, but for me the air leaked out of that particular balloon that night. I had made a timorous effort to insert myself into things, but could never shake the feeling of being somehow too odd, too inhibited, too gay, or too boringly intellectual for people to really accept me.

The Bryson was undergoing unpleasant changes, another sign of things drawing to some conclusion. Stephanie was fired. The building owners installed a preposterous couple, a pair of nosy, creepily Norman Rockwell–looking Okies to run the hotel. Ignorant, malevolent Dust Bowl hicks from central casting: a skinny crone with a sharp, evil face and her dithering, flatulent husband. They weren't even *Californian* Okies, but the genuine article, grafted from some invasive vegetable species in the high-wheat country directly onto the furniture behind the reception desk. (The tableau they presented every day in the lobby was reproduced note-perfectly in *The Grifters* thirteen years later—even more weirdly, the bizarre shotgun accident depicted at the beginning of *Magnolia* occurs through what used to be my living room window at the Bryson.)

Proposition 13, also known as the Jarvis-Gann Initiative—also known, hilariously, as "People's Initiative to Limit Property Tax"—was thought certain to pass when it came up for a vote the following spring. This ballot referendum, contrived to enrich the already rich but relentlessly advertised as a benefit to all, would freeze California property taxes at their current figure. As a sop to the non-rich, rents were supposed to be rolled back to their next-previous amount.

In anticipation, landlords made flimsy cosmetic tweaks that could then be claimed as substantial renovations that justified a rent increase: when rents were rolled back, they would only be lowered to what they'd been before the plumbing got fixed or the boiler replaced. The Okies had been brought in partly to oversee the nonexistent improvements, but also to drive out as many tenants as possible.

They set about it with malicious glee, selectively withholding tenants' mail and, though it could never be proved, throwing it away. They targeted pensioners and welfare dependents who'd lived in the Bryson forever. I got a Legal Aid lawyer to file a complaint with the post office, but the result—the installation of actual mailboxes with locks in the lobby—supposedly qualified as a rent-hiking property improvement. Next, the elevator stopped working, on a semi-permanent basis, supposedly shut down for repair. Finally, the malignant new managers began letting themselves into apartments with a passkey when the tenants were out, allegedly inspecting for leaks and damaged furnishings.

I kept a bowl of loose change in my kitchen. One day the Okie woman stopped me in the lobby.

"You know, you shouldn't keep all that money lying around your apartment where someone could steal it."

It was infuriating to picture this malicious hag inspecting my personal things, but the Okies were impervious to insults or threats. I had already arranged with a friend of Ferd's to steal all the furniture in the lobby the following evening and sell it at the Rose Bowl Flea Market, so I kept my mouth shut.

I loved living at the Bryson. For a few years, at least, it was one of those rare places exempt from the passage of time, like certain islands and barren landscapes in the north and bankrupt cities where industry has come and gone and won't return. Now it was all going to change, swiftly and horribly. I lit an imaginary candle before bed and prayed for Fred MacMurray to die.

La Rochefoucauld: Il arrive quelquefois des accidents dans la vie d'où il faut être un peu fou pour se bien tirer.

fifteen

Ricardo, my new boyfriend, drags me to visit Ino, who teaches dance. Ino lives in a gigantic five-story building between the Capitolio and the Plaza de Armas. The entrance is like the mouth of a whale, a pitch-black tunnel between the sidewalk and a courtyard where laundry hangs from sagging balconies overhead and everything visible looks theatrically battered and decrepit, the set of an imaginary Samuel Beckett opera directed by Visconti.

Cement steps on the left go to a mezzanine terrace of apartment doors, balustrades, a restaurant with little tables planted in the walkway, dwarfed by the vaulted underside of the floor above. Across the mezzanine, a staircase of wooden slats grooved with rot bypasses the upper floors to the roof. Ino's room resembles the shack Monica Vitti's friends demolish for firewood in *Red Desert*. It has a water closet, no bath. He washes in the sink. The floor feels stable, but really the whole Piranesian structure could collapse in a second into a pile of debris, as old buildings in Havana often do.

The roof is a sky-shantytown of hovels, like animal burrows, lining an alley of packed earth. Instead of doors they have gauze, with Santeria candles flickering on altars to the Black Virgin of Regla behind them. I'm not convinced that the science fiction effect of Ino's roof—the Capitolia dome, copied from the US Capitol Building, looms gigantically and looks about to collide, like the rogue planet in *Melancholia*—justifies the risk of plunging to a certain skull fracture by setting foot on Ino's staircase. Ino is a florid, sweaty, histrionic queen, who throws his meaty arms around me and kisses my face unpleasantly whenever he remembers I'm in the room. This is the third or fourth time I've visited Ino with Ricardo. I've tried hard to like him, but don't really.

Ino always has boys from the country in his cluttered lair, who sit or stand around looking spellbound until Ino sends them bolting down to fetch something from outside. Sometimes it's another boy or a melon or a bottle of Havana Club. He finds these boys nearby, in front of Kid Chocolate Boxing Hall, where they gravitate upon arrival. Ino ensorcells them with eccentricity and bits of food. They expect a little cash from anyone they sleep with—rightly so, if it's a tourist. Even rich Cubans are poor compared with tourists, and any foreigner in Cuba is richer than a poor Cuban. I don't know if Ino pays them, or just lets them use his bed for business transactions. I can't imagine where he goes in that event or if he stays and watches or joins in.

★

I'm behind the wheel of a blue Mazda sedan on the Harbor Freeway in the early autumn of 1978. The extreme right lane of the Harbor Freeway, near the junction where the left lanes curve to negotiate an underpass. Every lane is marked off by speed bumps, raised metal cleats that rattle the car if you drive over them. Commuting from Watts to Westwood, I've developed the habit, or game really, of steering out of the far right lane at the last possible moment,

GARY INDIANA   217

as the freeway widens and divides, into the farthest left
lane, crossing six lanes of traffic, the object being to avoid
all speed bumps. A real test of dexterity. The Mazda glides
into the underpass, hugging the extreme left curve of the
freeway as the road skirts the huge cement pylons that
support the Hollywood Freeway overhead. A game of skill
and daring, and fabulous stupidity.

Something is wrong with the car. It hawks and splutters
when I turn the ignition. The engine slacks for a couple
beats during a gear shift, as if a nonexistent fan belt has
slipped off—the car doesn't have a fan belt. When I bought
it, I was mildly interested to learn the Mazda rotary engine
was "all one piece," more dramatically so than a normal
car engine. If one component broke, the whole engine
became worthless. I couldn't imagine anything going wrong
with such a car. I assumed it would one day die a natural
death and possibly shoot up into the upper air, in a sort of
Auto Rapture.

Events, or a lack of them, have instilled in me an
unshakeable sense of utter insignificance. I am too peculiar
to figure importantly in anyone's life, including my own.
Even years later, when the idea that I exist can be asserted
with external evidence—books I've published, films I've
acted in, plays I've directed, friends who can confirm my
physical reality, passport records of countries I've visited,
bank statements, dental records, blood test results,
psychiatric files, hotel registers, airline ticket stubs, old
photos, bales of early writing archived at a major university,
and other documentary proof—I will continue to register
as a blurry human smudge in my mind's eye.

But now, in 1978, I'm trading the Mazda for a used,
dusty VW Bug at a dealership in Glendale. I drive off the
lot with unnerving clumsiness, having lost the hang of

operating a stick shift. The car lurches up an on-ramp into seething west-bound traffic. I'm keenly conscious that my cousin Jimmy died only three years ago in a crash of exactly this model Volkswagen. The engine punched through his back. I recall a well-intended but vulgar, tactless remark my father made at the funeral. I briefly despise him for it, then cringe guiltily for my punitive thoughts about this parent, whose life hasn't been any picnic, whose own parents knee-capped his self-estimation like two Mafia thugs from day one. They fuck you up, your mum and dad. They may not mean to, but they do. The car stinks of sour dust and motor oil. Fetid after languishing unloved for months, between more attractive, sexier, younger vehicles, under wire lines of flapping plastic pennants. I have an eerie fantasy that I'm driving the death car my cousin was crushed in.

Over the ensuing days, minor accidents in the VW cause me to regret the trade-in. I crash the front bumper into the wall of the Bryson garage. In Chatterton's back lot, the rear bumper collides, with great force, into a parking meter. The car's steering is tight as a spool of thread, the tires instantly pivot when I touch the steering wheel. The gas, clutch, and brake pedals feel too close together, or too far apart. I swerve out of lane on the 101 and miss scraping a tanker truck by a hair. The car seems scarily vulnerable, like a brittle shell between me and highway fatality.

On the weekend, Dane, who recently ditched me in the Spike to pick up a comelier trick, insists I come to the house in the Valley, where cardboard boxes he didn't unpack for three years have been joined by many others containing everything he did unpack. He pours shots from a Sambuca bottle. He's moving ahead with leaving town, depressingly cheerful, promising he'll stay in touch, which he won't.

He interrupts his clearing out to waltz-walk me into the
bedroom. "Maybe," he says, exposing Mr. Stiffy in friendly
tumescence, "you'll come to Austin some time." "Not real
likely," I say. "If you come," he says in what he thinks is a
Texas accent, "I'll fuck you real good."
We have sadly self-conscious sex, stopping often to
drink more Sambuca and smoke cigarettes. We're both
elsewhere. I'm impatient to finish and leave. Dane isn't
planning to depart for another two weeks, but I'm not
emotionally equipped to return again, to an even more
vacant house, which already has the hangover vibe of a
struck theater set after closing night.
On Sunday, Ferd calls and chats for an hour before
carefully disclosing that he's moving back to Chicago. I
can hear that he knew this news would upset me and
avoided telling me for a long time. I pretend I'm not
bothered. My instinct is to berate myself for feeling
anything, as if my ordinary emotions are irrelevant. Ferd
argued with himself, he says, until yesterday, that he ought
to tough it out, move to his own LA apartment, but he
doesn't see any bright future in California.
"I didn't realize you were expecting a bright future,"
I said.
"Of course I'm not," he says. "You know what I'm saying.
If I stay I'll get a shitty job I hate, and muddle around for
another decade. How's that working for you?"
"Thanks for reminding me."
"You'd feel more secure, and also more free, if you lived
closer to your family, wouldn't you?"
"In Boston? Ferd, fuck that. You know? Fuck that. You
plan to spend a lot of time with your dad in Alpena?"
"No. But I got offered a gig at that Latino high school,
why not do it for a while? It'll make a change. It isn't a

leap in the void."

"If I leave, the only logical place would be New York. I can't live in Boston again. People rot away there. It's totally inert."

"This commune isn't working out," Ferd says, not for the first time. They haven't blown up a building or kidnapped an oil company CEO or carried out any other murderous pipe dreams worth going underground for, though they've all behaved as if they were on the Most Wanted List for over a year. He is, he says, rethinking Leninism, "and the whole base and superstructure paradigm."

"I thought that was Stalin's idea," I say. "I read Comrade Stalin's thinking on base and superstructure not long ago. On your recommendation, come to think of it."

"Read *Mansfield Park* instead. It's more true to life. This has been like Stalinism without Stalin."

"I used to think you'd make a good Stalin, Ferd. But I've judged you too harshly, probably."

Ferd suspects the commune will soon breed Golden Labs and hold bake sales in the front yard. He's decided, finally, he's going to bury himself for now, teaching high school to Hispanic inner-city youths. He will fan the flames of revolution on weekends, if he isn't too exhausted.

Carol phones days later, with similar tidings. She's set on leaving UCSB for Pima College in Tucson, where they've offered her a job. Carol has history in Tucson, I recall, unless her tales from yesteryear of hanging around Andy Warhol while he shot *Lonesome Cowboys* was another Carol fabrication. The thought of living in the desert gives me creeps.

No contact with savage Indian tribes has ever daunted me more than the morning I spent with an old lady swathed in woolies, who compared herself to a rotten herring encased in a block of ice: she appeared intact, she said, but was threatened with disintegration, if her protective envelope should happen to melt.

—*Claude Lévi-Strauss,* Tristes Tropiques

sixteen

There has been no butter for two weeks. A taxi driver thought there might be butter in the supermarket in Miramar. I think so too: I once saw a man in that market buy twenty cases of Coca-Cola in loose twelve-ounce plastic bottles. Otherwise there is no butter to be found anywhere in Havana. I am not going to Miramar to find butter. I am content to believe I could, whereas I'd be most unhappy if I went and discovered they didn't have any.

Last week there were no tomatoes. We looked for them everywhere, to make spaghetti sauce. Just when we resigned ourselves to no tomatoes ever again, the markets were suddenly full of them. Things like this happen all the time. Yesterday our building elevator, broken since the rains in May, was repaired. We rushed out for the joy of returning later and making out with our dates in the elevator. Or with each other, if we didn't find dates.

There is now a shortage of pharmaceuticals. That is the embargo. I have an infection. First the national pharmacies ran out of Dipirona for pain. Then Cipro disappeared. In the full-price international pharmacy in Miramar a tall, fortyish Jewish Cuban American princess held up the line for forty minutes with the kind of obnoxious, trivial complaint visiting Cuban Americans love to inflict on people working here in stores, smugly aware that they are inconveniencing many of their former countrymen by exploiting the bureaucratic fastidiousness and imperturbable slow pace of the people serving them. The proud little smile this witch offered the twelve people waiting behind her reminded me for all the world of an erstwhile editor of mine, a malignant twat who was full of absurdly unmerited self-confidence and had the brains of a luncheon menu. I gave the woman in the pharmacy the finger, which happened to be the infected one. I've just given the editor the same finger, so I suppose this infection is good for something.

The orthopedist at the university hospital wanted me to take Cipro for five days before he lanced the blistered fingertip, which everyone on the Malecón is curious about now, as it began as a tiny white discoloration and quickly blossomed into a major problem. Also, since it was soaked in iodine, the bandage looks like a little orange microphone for Karaoke Barbie. But after two days I couldn't stand it. We went to see Ricardo's mother's cousin who works in a hospital lab across the road from the Carlos III shopping center. She walked us through a maze of hospital corridors and waiting areas, some of them open to the sky, to a doctor who told her to poke it open with a sterile needle and squeeze the pus out, which Ricardo's mother's cousin proceeded to do, while a lab worker on maternity leave came by to show off her new baby. I wanted to scream from pain but didn't. I looked at the baby and saw a future of scrapes and bruises. Life is short and full of pain and always beautiful, besides.

My Santeria doctor thinks he can cure anything. He is useless for anything besides back problems, where he does possess a certain genius. Even then, he insists on explaining "the Eastern philosophy" he studies, at such tedious length

that what are basically chiropractic sessions are ten percent treatment and ninety percent explanation of how the blood flows around the brain when the chakras or whatever are in tune with the moon. I get a brand-new pain from nodding like a moron for forty minutes out of sixty. All the same, I call him to give me acupressure with a lit taper, which distracts me from my finger.

At the original hospital, a different orthopedist, young and handsome, studies the result of my treatment at the second hospital. He decides to scalpel away the blister, scrape out the infection, and douse the wound with iodine. First he injects a local that numbs my other fingers and leaves the afflicted one with full sensation. So that little operation was a trip. Now the finger is only a little swollen, but I can't get it wet. The surgical glove they gave me to wear in the shower doesn't fit over the bandage. We wanted to go to Camagüey and swim in the coral reef. Now we can't do it until August, if I come back in August. You must never plan, is the lesson here. Last year all the raving beauties on the Malecón were from Isla de la Juventud, but this month they are all from Camagüey. We thought it would be nice to meet some who hadn't moved to Havana and become complete whores yet. It has to wait.

★

Tuesday night, the Westland Twins: we're screening a stupendously dull Claude Lelouch flick, *If I Had to Do It All Over Again*. Between show times, Kevin and I restock the candy shelves, tart up the refreshment area, tally sales, and gurgle a little song: "If I had to do it all over again, I'd do it all over you!" Kevin needs a ride home to Venice after work. He invites me to check out some gay bars on the way to his house. This is the first time we've gone drinking. Also the last, as it turns out.

The beachside bars have nautical or underwater themes. Unlike gay bars in the city, which all imitate cowboy movie saloons, these shine with polished aquariums and glossy plants and smell like ozone. They have an unpleasant trick of using pinkish flood lamps to achieve the same degree of visual obscurity as bars that are semidark. Instead of torpor, though, these places encourage hyperanimation. Cruising guys dart at their intended prey in brusque strides, venture a few hurried words, speed to their next prospect when deflected. It's as if the lugubrious, defensive ritual of snuffling for cock has been revamped as a wacky, tacky afternoon game show.

Evidently, Venice bars all contain the same twenty or thirty muscular, blond, ex- or current gay surfers, each bent on coupling with his twin, or with an equally svelte, chiseled, darker version of himself with black hair and an Italian or Jewish nose. The seaside prime meat are disco queens with class pretentions, a whole species apart from the horny supermarket stock boys, civilian leather tops, and grungily alluring ex-convicts I readily attract in East Hollywood. This bunch looks aggressively brainless as they ardently appraise each other's bracelets, shoes, haircuts, and other signs of expensive maintenance. They speak a metallic birdsong of sun and surf. In another time and place, their tribe would be easily enslaved through the judicious gifting of cowrie shells and glass trinkets. They boast of sultry lives, careers in jewelry design and hairdressing. They hint that they're kept playthings of multimillionaires away on business. Chatter is all soigné weekends in Cabo and St. Barts, blunt-force fucking that's better than sex because it has money mixed in with it. In ten years, all these people will be dead, since the exaggeratedly attractive are first to go in the epidemic.

Kevin hurls himself into the fray, circumnavigating the bar with breezy smiles, unfazed by the lack of attention he's getting. I see straight off he isn't made for these places: he's short, incipiently potbellied, overly fem, his cuteness

dissolves into facelessness beside so much fashion perfection. I know I'm too skinny and mentally complicated, too lacking in muscle tone, too neurotic to elicit any interest, and focus on drinking. I seldom smile. When these camera-ready types ever speak to me at all, it's to say that I look sad, tell me to cheer up, as if the way my face settles threatens their world view. I can't feature hooking up with any of these bitchy, emotionless Creatures of the Beach, even if they wanted to. At least with an ex-convict, there's a little damaged tenderness.

We can't peel free of these bars. Venice has many. When we exit one, Kevin remembers another. He's obsessed with getting dick. Of course it has to belong to a real beauty. He clocks every godlike underwear model on entering a place, makes a beeline for the most impossibly hot one, then the runner-up, and third place, ultimately exposing himself to rejection by the consolation prize—buys them drinks, laughs at their idiocies, flatters them, flirts, gets exactly nowhere but presses on undaunted, circling over now and then to keep me up to speed with his progress. He's determined to hook up with the unattainable, I think, to make me believe it's what he normally gets. If I weren't around, he'd probably settle for a perfectly nice, plain-looking schlub—there are a few, scattered around, abjectly nursing lonely beers.

Naturally we're drinking, a lot, gin and tonics, drinking to sustain an attitude of superiority in the face of all the nasty reception he's getting. Even I draw pitying looks in these shitholes, and I'm conspicuously *not* checking anyone out, or even looking at them. I can't believe Kevin doesn't know how misplaced he looks among perfect bodies with perfect faces who've spent all day adoring themselves in mirrors. I'm not sure he understands how banal all their preening perfection is, either. But eventually, as one o'clock arrives, he becomes palpably frustrated, even petulant. He

scowls at his failed conquests as they pair off with one other.
After the fourth bar, it occurs to me that I'm wasted. I see
triple unless I squint. But I'm beyond prudence. I let him
talk me into a nightcap, at yet another gay dump.

It's a cramped, crowded joint, more like the familiar meat
racks on Santa Monica Boulevard. I seize an empty barstool
and order . . . a Southern Comfort, for some reason, while
Kevin, hope springing eternal again, canvases the detritus
. . . my back to the room, my eyelids droop shut and I slip
into momentary unconsciousness, then jerk awake forgetting
where I am and how I got here. This mystery only fully
clears up when Kevin swims into view, en route to another
prospective turndown. I go out of consciousness several
times. It's scary, I'm absent only a couple seconds but then
it feels like days have passed when I refocus the room and
the men crammed into it.

I find Kevin after several micro-naps, to tell him I'm
leaving. I'll drop him off, unless he wants to find his own
way home.

"Naah, I'm wrecked . . ."

In the car, he veils his disappointment with bright, queeny
chatter, about nothing whatsoever. I consider asking if I can
sleep on his couch, but it's possible he doesn't have one,
and it might be freaky to wake up next to Kevin in the
morning. I can only drive with one eye shut. I pull up to his
building.

"Are you okay to drive?"

"I think so."

"Okay, then, see you at the theater . . ."

As I drive away I haven't a clue where the freeway is.
There's always one when you don't need one, so there has
to be one somewhere. Trusting my sense of direction, which
doesn't exist, I get lost on surface roads for an hour. It's as

if neighborhoods shift around a la *Dark City*, planting themselves in my path a few seconds ahead of me, after I've already driven through them. I discover I've navigated in a circle of several miles' circumference, suddenly arriving again at Kevin's house. I'm tempted to park nearby and sleep in the car. Scouting a suitable alley, the nose of the Volkswagen unexpectedly picks up the scent of a freeway on-ramp.

In my own mind, at least, this will be a straight shot to the Rampart Street off-ramp and the Wilshire District. The freeways are practically forlorn at this hour. The road and all I can see from it has the desolate look everything in Los Angeles has after midnight, when the epic space the city occupies reveals its human-shrinking emptiness.

The ribbon of the empty road releases an ectoplasmic copy of itself as the car passes over it. Gusts of foggy mist sweep across the blurry lanes, like spectral tumbleweed. Some headlights on the southbound lanes glare across my windshield. In no time, a cluster of twinkling downtown towers appears on the right. I brace for the upcoming divide of the 101. Opening both eyes, I see sixteen lanes instead of eight. I'm not sure which eye to trust.

Despite the nervous responsiveness of the VW's steering, my habitual contest with the freeway system eliminates all sense of caution. With a brainless feeling of mastery, I prod the wheel left, quickly pull right, back left, back right, executing a brilliantly supple, snakelike, diagonal line across all eight lanes without grazing a single speed bump.

Then, as if an insensible number of frames have been spliced from a movie I'm watching, the car slides into the underpass to the Hollywood Freeway, instantly skidding insanely back and forth. Yanking the wheel sends it into an uncontrollable zigzag between the massive pylons holding up the Hollywood Freeway. In a flash of grotesque literary reflection, I recall the final paragraph of *A Charmed Life*, where Mary McCarthy's heroine smashes head on into another car: as the fatal collision occurs, she has a second in which to realize that, in the town she's living in, this wouldn't be happening if she had been driving, as everyone did there at that hour, on the wrong side of the road.

I'm going to die now, I think. It's my last lucid thought for a while. Miraculously, the VW clears the underpass without guidance, but after rounding the corner careens straight up the embankment, flips over, flips over again, teeters on two wheels, completes a final flip, and settles upside down with a sickening thud, a foot or two shy of the road surface.

Strapped in the bucket seat, I contemplate a strange view of torn-up ice plant and gnarled embankment through the shattered, upside down windshield. My head has smashed against numerous surfaces in spite of the seat belt. I test myself for brain damage. I conjugate several French verbs. I struggle to recall the specific year of General Gordon's siege of Khartoum. I grope around for the door handle. It falls off. Unclasping the seat belt, I test my limbs for mobility. My entire body feels damaged, but after much probing around seems miraculously intact. I crawl out the upside down window.

Crouching in the stubbly ice plant, it occurs to me that I might spend the night in jail. No, I won't, I vow, forcing my grudging limbs and the rest of me to crawl further uphill, until I manage to stand and climb to the upper lip of the embankment. In what you could truly call a leap of faith, I scramble over the retaining wall, and drop several feet to the shoulder of the Hollywood Freeway—which has traffic moving on it, and looks like foolproof suicide to cross.

In an onrush of complete idiocy, I sprint across gaps in

several lanes of angry headlights, reaching the other side in a fanfare of enraged horns, feeling mid-freeway that something's broken or ruptured below my ribs.

On the other side, a steep escarpment rises from a narrow, eerily vacant street way below, in a neighborhood, if it is one, that I guess to be somewhere between the Rampart District and Echo Park. An unknown area that passes in a blink if you're driving, but stretches for miles through alien terrain if you're not. Every part of Los Angeles is like that: things that appear close through your windshield are really puzzlingly far away.

A half hour later, I've stumbled and slid down a crumbling declivity of rocks and dirt. The street at the bottom traverses a malignant-looking neighborhood of scattered two-story houses festering in dark overgrowths of vegetation, none showing any lights or evidence of occupancy.

I slog off in a tentatively western direction. When I consider that I should have died an hour earlier, a Valium calm flushes through me. Single-mindedly intent on hobbling all the way to the Bryson Apartments, miles from here for all I know, my idea is: if I make it home, and sleep, and sober up, if my face isn't a bruised pulp in the morning, I might get away with claiming I was home all night, that the car was stolen from the Bryson garage. I don't know anything about it getting wrecked beside the freeway . . . yes, exactly, but then . . . the California Highway Patrol can check the car registration from the plates in fifteen seconds, find out where I live, for all I know they're waiting to surprise me in the Bryson lobby already. I could hide somewhere until I sober up. I'll tell the cops I spent the night at a friend's house. But I would've taken the car, in that case. Anyway, where do I imagine I can sleep? If I hide behind one of these houses, an alarm could go off, some property owner might come out with a shotgun.

Suddenly the fact that every inch of this city is somebody's private property makes the inspiration doubtful. I could call Dane. Ask him to rescue me. Except I don't know where I am. I don't know his number by heart, either, and don't have my phone book. Furthermore, there's no phone anywhere. If he came, I could stay with him. Except he might have already left town. If he's still around, though, I could tell the police I was out of town when my car was stolen. "I only found out about it now, officer . . ." No, it's hopeless and stupid.

An hour passes. I am still trudging down the dark road, through endless nothingness. Potholes scar the street, grass pokes up where tar has fissured and crumbled away. The street doesn't end, doesn't connect to anything, it's a hateful, stupid cancerous-looking black tongue lapping the earth's surface for miles, in a wasteland without a speck of life except an occasional flickering street lamp and invisible dogs barking in darkness. No view, a monotony of abandoned houses and weed-infested driveways. I'm going to get nailed by the law, or become the first male victim of the Hillside Strangler, or swallowed by this sinkhole of a neighborhood.

After hours . . . up a small hill . . . at an empty intersection . . . a gas station! A large! Bright! Gas station! Where nobody's minding the store: four banks of Serv-Ur-Self gas pumps with spread-out fluorescent bat wings anchored twenty feet above them. A phone booth glows at the edge of the tar piazza. I abandon my impossible quest to reach the Bryson. Peering in all four directions, I don't recognize a single feature of the neighborhood. All right. I surrender. I step into the phone booth. I fish a quarter from my pants. I call the police.

They show up in four patrol cars, sirens shrieking. Seven officers jump out of the cruisers with their guns drawn and surround the phone booth. There's a lot of rough language, conveying their anger and disgust at my irresponsibility. There's a pinch of homophobic ridicule, but not as much as I might have expected. They look me over, frisk me for weapons and drugs, then grill me about my employment status. They ask where I live, though they already know. They want to know if I have accident insurance. I do. They conclude that I'm harmless.

They say they've already inspected the car. They were able to tell by the torn-up ground cover how many times it rolled over. It's the kind of accident, they assure me, almost with admiration, that absolutely no one walks out of alive. One middle-aged guy with a kinder manner than the others, an avuncular sort, advises that I should thank whoever's up there—he indicates outer space with his finger—that I'm not paralyzed with a broken spine or blind or dead, because I really should be.

Since I did walk away from it, and because it's the 1970s, before Mothers Against Drunk Driving turned drunk driving into the moral equivalent of serial pedophilia and murder even when nobody gets hurt, the cops don't arrest me on a DUI. They don't even take me in to file an accident report. "Even though I can see you're wasted," one of them grumbles, "nobody's dead, seems like you came out of it okay—it's basically a waste of our time to take this any further."

I'm not entirely free to go, but I'm not under arrest. Instead, he says, I must wait here for a tow truck they've already called, and accompany the tow-truck driver to the scene of the crash, then ride with him and the smashed-up VW to the city impound. I can reclaim the car after three days, if I pay the towing and storage charges.

The tow-truck driver is totally nonjudgmental about the whole thing. He's obviously pleased to get business thrown his way at such a late hour. He's about fifty, mildly

overweight, with a face like a peeled apple, wearing overalls
and cowboy boots.

"You lucked out," he assures me, "on account of you've
got the insurance. No insurance, you'd be spending the
night in the holding tank."

En route to the impound, we pass through a bosky
Mexican neighborhood lined with broken street lamps where
people are still on the sidewalks in front of their houses, a
pickup basketball game parting like the Red Sea for the
truck to pass through it.

"Plus you're white," the driver adds. "With cops in this
town, that's one lucky plus."

The next day, bruises covered me from about the sternum
to my shins. I was too lame to walk. But I had nothing broken,
no concussion, and cabbed to a doctor who told me to stay in
bed for a few days and I would be, in his words, "good to go."

I was good to go, I realized. Once I got my bearings, I
understood that commuting to Watts on a city bus and
arranging how to get to Westwood at the end of the day, and
home at the end of the night, was a step too far down the
ladder, into the basement of the City of Dreams reserved
for cashiered starlets and sad fixtures in piano bars who
once upon a time had "been somebody." I had never been
anybody, and if I stayed in LA, I realized, I never would be.

I interpreted the accident as a sign. Not a sign from
God, who, unless he's truly the worst prick in the universe,
doesn't exist. It was a sign from an enormous, disembodied,
imaginary fuck-you finger poking through "a dense gray
cloud of you'll never know."

I packed my typewriter, clothes, a few books, and stashed
the rest of my stuff in a storage loft at Chatterton's. A week
later, I took a cab to the airport. I had forty dollars, a TWA
Getaway Card, and a friend's address in New York.

Epilogue

I went back to the island for a few days, to see Ricardo: the worst possible time, as it turned out, Havana being overrun by American tourists set loose by newly relaxed travel restrictions. Alberto sold the apartment on 21 y G "out from under me"—we'll never have that ideal place again, and the generically acceptable flat Ricardo reserved became suddenly unavailable hours before my arrival. We ended up in a dreary warren in Vedado during a bizarre four-day cold snap that kept us indoors, in a freezing bedroom, huddled under thin blankets, without much to say to each other and with nothing whatever to distract us. A true nadir: We spent many hours trying to force ourselves to sleep at times when we would normally set out for a night's chance encounters and a bit of fun.

No doubt everything will change, some time, but for now most of what I've loved here has turned sour or disappeared. The Bim Bom scene was dispersed a few seasons ago by the placement of floodlights aimed at the sidewalks around the cafetería. The same has happened along the Malecón, with the installation of blinding lamps on the thruway divider. Nobody gathers there (or anywhere else) any more— except the incongruous guests of the Hotel Nacional, who're ecstatic to photograph themselves in front of the sea wall and parade through the city on the open decks of tour buses, like an army of triumphant vandals. If anything, the improbable numbers of these new visitors has amped up the vigilance of the police, who interfere with any Cuban they see in company with any foreigner.

It simply isn't possible to continue things as we've done for so long, hiring cars to take us anywhere we need to go together, or walking ten feet apart in the street, continually scanning for cops. There is practically nowhere left to go, in any case: The gay bar an Italian opened on Humboldt Street a year ago has been shut down "for drugs," the Echeverria disco and its palm-studded, walled grounds is likewise kaput; all that remains is Toke, a snack bar–restaurant adjacent to the dreaded Las Vegas Club, its patio tables on Infanta Street cruised all night by a shifting assortment of out-and-out hustlers on the sidewalk, who all look like they just got out of jail.

The city feels shrunken, like a decrepit resort town full of long-shuttered attractions. A scattering of new, slightly-better-than-the-usual restaurants offers occasional queasy relief (but no culinary excitement) from the Apartheid-like constriction that dictates our time together. Ricardo is a kind of partner, but really just a friend. An intimate friend I feel vaguely responsible for. Whatever watery plans we once devised to get him away from Cuba have gradually evaporated. He doesn't really want to leave: He just wants to secure a different nationality, as immunity against police harassment. (He's the furthest thing from a criminal or a hustler imaginable, but his deep-black skin color makes him a favored target for the city's criminal peacekeepers, who are mainly light brown or off-white.) This is something I can't accomplish for him, given the Byzantine immigration laws of my country. And I can't keep returning here. While writing my book in Alberto's dream flat, all the circumstances that make life here meager and depressing were manageable, even easy to ignore: the cops, the boredom, the perpetual shortages of food items and medicines. But the book is finished, and the soft brutality of island communism has become unbearable. Ricardo is better off without a companion whose very presence makes him an object of negative scrutiny.

The book: It has turned out radically different than I expected. At some point I began to prune away anything suggesting the sort of "triumph over adversity" theme that gongs through much of the so-called memoir genre, paring away most evidence of my eventual career as a writer and artist—which has not, in any case, been an unmitigated triumph over adversity. I'm almost sixty-five, I still have practically nothing of my own, and could very well end up on the same trash heap where most old people in America get tossed, regardless of whatever "cultural capital" I've accumulated.

Eventually I let go of any pretense of documentary reality, and kept instead the evocation of things happening to a person for the first time, of being young and completely unprepared for life. This inevitably brought Ferd Eggan into it more conspicuously than a different vector of narrative would have. I see that I've concluded it when Ferd and I separately departed Los Angeles in 1978. That was hardly the end of our dealings, though we had no contact at all for almost a decade; on a book tour for my first novel, I spent some days in Chicago, and suddenly there he was again. After that we stayed in touch, sometimes cohabited, a few times traveled together; I haven't told the story of his life here, but rather the part of it that repeatedly intersected with mine. Ferd really deserves his own book; someone else will have to write it.

Seven Stories Press
140 Watts Street
New York, NY 10013
www.sevenstories.com

Library of Congress Cataloging-in-Publication Data is on file.

ISBN: 978-1-64421-389-6 (paperback)
ISBN: 978-1-64421-390-2 (ebook)

College professors and high school and middle school teachers may order free examination copies of Seven Stories Press titles. Visit https://www.sevenstories.com/pg/resources-academics or email academic@sevenstories.com.

Printed in the United States of America

9 8 7 6 5 4 3 2 1